S. HRG. 113–200

S. 980—THE EMBASSY SECURITY AND PERSONNEL PROTECTION ACT OF 2013

HEARING

BEFORE THE

COMMITTEE ON FOREIGN RELATIONS
UNITED STATES SENATE

ONE HUNDRED THIRTEENTH CONGRESS

FIRST SESSION

JULY 16, 2013

Printed for the use of the Committee on Foreign Relations

Available via the World Wide Web: http://www.gpo.gov/fdsys/

U.S. GOVERNMENT PRINTING OFFICE

86–864 PDF   WASHINGTON : 2014

For sale by the Superintendent of Documents, U.S. Government Printing Office
Internet: bookstore.gpo.gov   Phone: toll free (866) 512–1800; DC area (202) 512–1800
Fax: (202) 512–2104   Mail: Stop IDCC, Washington, DC 20402–0001

(II)

CONTENTS

(III)

S. 980—THE EMBASSY SECURITY AND PERSONNEL PROTECTION ACT OF 2013

TUESDAY, JULY 16, 2013

U.S. SENATE,
COMMITTEE ON FOREIGN RELATIONS,
Washington, DC.

The committee met, pursuant to notice, at 10:03 a.m., in room SD–419, Dirksen Senate Office Building, Hon. Robert Menendez (chairman of the committee) presiding.

Present: Senators Menendez, Cardin, Murphy, Kaine, Corker, Flake, and Barrasso.

OPENING STATEMENT OF HON. ROBERT MENENDEZ, U.S. SENATOR FROM NEW JERSEY

The CHAIRMAN. This hearing of the Senate Foreign Relations Committee will come to order.

Today, our real focus is ensuring the security of our missions abroad and the safety of our Foreign Service personnel. That has always been, and will remain, a priority of this committee.

Having said that, I hope to have the support of my Republican colleagues for The Embassy Security Act I have introduced, named for Chris Stevens, Sean Smith, Tyrone Woods, and Glen Doherty, who gave their lives in service to the Nation in Benghazi on September the 11th. The lessons we have learned from the tragedies in Nairobi, Dar es Salaam, and Benghazi are emblematic of the broader issue we will increasingly face in the 21st century, and it will require our full, unequivocal, unwavering commitment to fully protect our embassies and those who serve this Nation abroad.

We have studied what went wrong, we have looked back, and now it is time to look forward and do what needs to be done to prevent another tragedy in the future. After Benghazi, the ARB made 29 recommendations to State and to Congress. While we must do our part in overseeing State's implementation, we must also do our part to provide the resources and necessary authorizations to ensure full implementation. And we must make whatever investments are necessary to protect our embassies and our missions.

Such investments are not an extravagance, they are not simply another budget item. We must strike the proper balance between sealing off vulnerabilities in high-threat areas and continuing to conduct vigorous and effective diplomacy that serves the national interests.

The fact is, we can never have absolute security in an increasingly dangerous world unless we hermetically seal our diplomats in steel tanks. But, security alone is not our objective. At the end of

(1)

the day, this is not an either/or choice. We need to address both the construction of new embassies that meet security needs, and we need to do what we can to ensure existing high-risk posts where we need our people to represent our interests and where new construction is not an option.

The ARB stated it clearly, ''The solution requires a more serious and sustained commitment from Congress to support State Department needs, which, in total, constitute a small percentage both of the full national budget and that spent for national security. One overall conclusion in this report is that Congress must do its part to meet this challenge and provide necessary resources to the State Department to address security risks and meet mission imperatives.''

The bill I have introduced as part of the solution, ''the serious and sustained commitment,'' it takes the lessons we have learned and turns them into action. As I said, total security is next to impossible. Our diplomats cannot encase themselves in stone fortresses and remain effective. And disengagement is clearly not an option. So, the solution must be multifaceted. It must include enhanced physical security around our embassies and ensure that our diplomats are equipped with the language skills and security training necessary to keep them safe when they come out from behind the embassy walls to do their jobs. It also requires us to ensure that the persons protecting our missions are not selected simply because they are the cheapest available force. Where conditions require enhanced security, this bill gives State additional flexibility to contract guard forces based on the best value rather than the lowest bidder.

It also means holding people accountable. When an employee exhibits unsatisfactory leadership that has serious security consequences, the Secretary must have the ability to act. This bill gives the Secretary greater flexibility in disciplinary actions in the future. It authorizes funding for key items identified by the Accountability Review Board on Benghazi, including embassy security and construction, Arabic language training, construction of a Foreign Affairs Security Training Center to consolidate and expand security training operations for State Department personnel so that, instead of piecing together our training and facilities up and down the East Coast, we streamline them in a single facility that can provide comprehensive training to more people.

And lastly, the bill requires detailed reports from the Department on its progress in implementing all of the recommendations made by the Accountability Review Board, and specifically requires the identification of, and reporting of, security at high-risk, high-threat facilities.

At the end of the day, if we fail to act, if we fail to address these issues, there will be another incident. The responsibility is ours, and the failure to act will be ours, as well. This is a time for solutions. The safety of those who serve this Nation abroad is in our hands.

With that, let me turn to my distinguished ranking colleague, who has worked with us to have this hearing, Senator Corker, for his opening statement.

OPENING STATEMENT OF HON. BOB CORKER, U.S. SENATOR FROM TENNESSEE

Senator CORKER. Well, thank you, Mr. Chairman. And thank you for your efforts to focus on the issue of embassy security and, candidly, just the way you conduct our efforts here in Foreign Relations in a bipartisan way. It is much appreciated.

And I want to thank the State Department for bringing forth the kind of witnesses that, you know, carry the weight on this issue that matters to all of us. So, thank you both for being here.

We have a procedural issue that is occurring at 11 o'clock that is semi-important. I may be stepping in and out on the phone, here, before that vote. But, I want to thank you both for being here. I know our offices have been in contact with you.

And let me just express a couple of concerns. I do not imagine there is anybody here that does not respect what our Foreign Service officers around the world do. And I think we all know, especially after what has happened in Libya, the threat that they are under. And we know those threats are taking place all over the world.

I know that the State Department has requested funding for numbers of new facilities that take many, many years to build, and yet, at the same time, I know we have people today in Peshawar and Harat, you know, where we just came from, or at least generally came from, that are under a lot of duress now and, candidly, you know, have some security issues. So, I do hope, as we move along, we will figure out a way to balance between some of the longer term projects that, candidly, are taking place not under very serious threat with some of the short-term needs that we have.

And I know there is also some focus on building a training facility, which I know is very expensive, and yet we are aware that maybe there are ways of doing that training in ways that do not require, you know, spending hundreds of millions of dollars to build it.

So, I just hope we will move along in an appropriate way. And I certainly do not want to rehash the past. I think the chairman knows we have tried to move away from some of the things that have happened in the past. But, I would like for somebody to explain to me, at some point, this ARB that we did have. I know we have four employees that were involved in, you know, some reporting on the ARBs. They are still on paid leave, and nothing has occurred. And I would like, at some point, to understand how we bring closure to that issue.

But, again, thank you both for being here. I thank you for your service to our country. And I hope, in a bipartisan way, we will move ahead in a way that certainly does the immediate things that are necessary to make sure that our Foreign Service officers are safe.

But, thank you.

The CHAIRMAN. Thank you.

I am pleased to introduce Bill Miller, the Deputy Assistant Secretary of State for High-Threat Posts, a new position created post-Benghazi. And we also have with us Gregory Starr, the Acting Assistant Secretary for Diplomatic Security and Director of the Diplomatic Security Service. These two officials sit at the nexus of policy development and management, and we look forward to hearing their perspective on this legislation and on the best way to secure our embassies and keep our personnel as safe as possible.

With our thanks for both of you being here, we will begin with your opening statements. Your full statements will be included in the record. We ask you to synthesize it in around 5 minutes or so, so we can have members engage with you in a dialogue.

STATEMENT OF GREGORY B. STARR, ACTING ASSISTANT SECRETARY FOR DIPLOMATIC SECURITY, PRINCIPAL DEPUTY ASSISTANT SECRETARY FOR DIPLOMATIC SECURITY, AND DIRECTOR OF THE DIPLOMATIC SECURITY SERVICE, U.S. DEPARTMENT OF STATE, WASHINGTON, DC

Mr. STARR. Thank you, Mr. Chairman, Ranking Member Corker. I want to thank you for your invitation to appear here today to discuss the future of embassy and diplomatic security.

We appreciate, and we share, your commitment to enhanced security, as evidenced in the recently introduced Chris Stevens, Sean Smith, Tyrone Woods, Glen Doherty Embassy Security and Personnel Protection Act of 2013.

The attacks on the U.S. diplomatic facilities last September, and subsequent attacks this year, as well, against diplomatic facilities and personnel remind us every day that the world is a dangerous place for diplomacy. Unfortunately, this is nothing new. Being on the front lines of U.S. national security has always been inherently risky. However, we strive to mitigate this risk to the maximum extent possible.

The fact remains that we will not, even with the most willing and capable government partners—as we have in many places around the world—we will not stop terrorists or extremists from attacking us in every instance. Rather, we must carefully balance this risk against the value of pursuing our national interests in these various countries. We have learned some very hard and painful lessons out of Benghazi. We are already acting on those lessons.

The State Department carries on the business of the American Government and its people in 284 locations, many in challenging security environments where key U.S. national security interests are at stake. Every day, the Department works to protect our people and missions by constantly assessing threats and our security posture overseas.

The Bureau of Diplomatic Security advances American interests and foreign policy by protecting people, property, and information. We do this by maintaining a security program that includes analyzing the threats, managing the security situation, and mitigating the risks.

DS constantly researches, monitors, and analyzes threats against Americans, our diplomatic facilities, and U.S. diplomatic personnel. This information, along with trend analysis and case studies of political violence, terrorist acts, and crime, form the basis of the threat assessments that we use that are provided to Department senior managers to support the operational and policy decision-making process. From this analysis, we determine what additional security measures, whether they be short term or long term, should be taken to mitigate the potential threats against our diplomatic assets.

From DS analysts in Washington, DC, monitoring the threats against our posts to our regional security officers abroad managing the security programs at these posts, we strive to provide the most secure platform for conducting American diplomacy. Building on the recommendations of the independent Benghazi Accountability Review Board, the interagency assessment teams that were sent out, and our own considerable experience and expertise, the Department is diligently working to improve the way we protect our diplomats, not only at our highest-threat posts, but at all of our facilities around the world.

Thanks, in large part, to your generous support in 2013 and the continuing resolution, progress is well underway. Pursuant to the recommendations of the independent Benghazi ARB, we are training more U.S. Foreign Affairs community personnel to deal with high-threat and high-risk environments through our Foreign Affairs counterthreat course. We are expanding the duration of DS high-threat tactical training courses, and incorporating elements of that training into other DS courses so that, regardless of a diplomatic securities special agent assignment, we have a flexible cadre of agents trained to operate in varying security environments overseas.

We are hiring 151 new security professionals this and next fiscal year—that is 151 total, not each year—many of whom will directly serve at, or provide support to, our high-threat, high-risk posts. We are also working very closely with the Department of Defense to expand the Marine Security Guard Program, as well as to enhance the availability of forces to respond, in extremis, to threatened U.S. personnel and facilities.

We recently worked with DOD and the U.S. Marine Corps to elevate personal security—the security that we provide for our people overseas—as a primary mission of the Marine Corps security guards. Each of these efforts enhances the Department's ability to supplement, as necessary, the host government's measures in fulfilling its obligations under international law to protect U.S. diplomats and consular property and personnel. The increased security funds you have provided will also support our colleagues at the Bureau of Overseas Building Operations in providing facilities for additional Marine security guard detachments, as well as the construction of new facilities and security-upgrade projects at some of our most critical posts.

The Bureau of Diplomatic Security realizes our work in securing our posts and protecting our people will never be done. We take great pride in our accomplishments. We apply the lessons learned, and we look forward to working with Congress on embassy security.

I recognize that my opening remarks are brief, because I wanted to allow plenty of time for questions, to answer your specific questions. I will be glad to take those questions after you have heard from my colleague Bill Miller, and he will provide his remarks at this point.

Thank you, Mr. Chairman. Thank you, Ranking Member Corker.

[The prepared statement of Mr. Starr follows:]

PREPARED STATEMENT OF GREGORY B. STARR

Good morning, Chairman Menendez, Ranking Member Corker, and distinguished committee members. Thank you for your invitation to appear here today to discuss the future of diplomatic security. We appreciate and share your commitment to enhanced embassy security as evidenced in the recently introduced "Chris Stevens, Sean Smith, Tyrone Woods, and Glen Doherty Embassy Security and Personnel Protection Act of 2013."

Today's Diplomacy

The attacks on U.S. diplomatic facilities last September, and subsequent attacks this year against diplomatic facilities and personnel, remind us that the world remains a dangerous place for diplomacy. Unfortunately, this is nothing new. Being on the front lines of U.S. national security has always been inherently risky; however, we strive to mitigate this risk to the maximum extent possible. The fact remains that we will not, even with the most willing and capable governments as our partners, stop terrorists or extremists from attacking us in every instance. Rather, we must carefully balance this risk against the value of pursuing our national interests. We have learned some very hard and painful lessons in Benghazi. We are already acting on them.

The State Department carries on the business of the American Government and its people at 284 locations, many in challenging security environments where key U.S. national security interests are at stake. Every day, the Department works to protect our people and missions by constantly assessing threats and our security posture. The Bureau of Diplomatic Security (DS) advances American interests and foreign policy by protecting people, property, and information. We do this by maintaining a security program that includes analyzing threats, managing the security situation, and mitigating risks.

Analyzing Threats

DS constantly researches, monitors, and analyzes threats against Americans, our diplomatic facilities, and U.S. diplomatic personnel. This information, along with trend analyses and case studies of political violence, terrorist acts, and crime form the basis of threat assessments that are provided to Department senior managers to support operational and policy decisionmaking. From this analysis, we determine what additional security measures, short-term or long-term, should be taken to mitigate potential threats against our diplomatic assets.

Managing the Security Environment and Mitigating Threats

From DS analysts in Washington, DC, monitoring threats against our posts to Regional Security Officers abroad managing security programs at those posts, we strive to provide the most secure platform for conducting American diplomacy. Building on the recommendations of the independent Benghazi Accountability Review Board, the Interagency Security Assessment Teams, and our own considerable experience and expertise, the Department is diligently working to improve the way we protect our diplomats not only at high-threat, high-risk posts but at all of our facilities worldwide.

Thanks in large part to your generous support in the FY 2013 Continuing Resolution, progress is well underway.

Pursuant to the recommendations of the independent Benghazi ARB, DS plans to train more of the U.S. foreign affairs community to deal with high-risk environments through our Foreign Affairs Counter-Threat course. We are expanding the duration of the DS high-threat tactical training course and incorporating elements of that training into other DS courses so that regardless of a DS special agent's assignment, we have a flexible cadre of agents trained to operate in varying security environments.

DS is hiring 151 new security professionals this and the next fiscal year, many of whom will directly serve at or provide support to our high-threat, high-risk posts. We are also working very closely with the Department of Defense (DOD) to expand the Marine Security Guard program, as well as to enhance the availability of forces to respond in extremis to threatened U.S. personnel and facilities. We recently worked with DOD and the U.S. Marine Corps to elevate personnel security as a primary mission of the Marine Security Guards. Each of these efforts enhances the Department's ability to supplement, as necessary, the host government's measures in fulfilling its obligations under international law to protect U.S. diplomatic and consular property and personnel.

The increased security funds you have provided will also support our colleagues at the Bureau of Overseas Buildings Operations in providing facilities for additional

Marine Security Guard Detachments, as well as the construction of new facilities and security upgrade projects at some of our most critical posts.

The Bureau of Diplomatic Security realizes our work in securing our posts and protecting our people will never be done. We take great pride in our accomplishments, apply lessons learned, and look forward to working with Congress on embassy security. I will be glad to answer any questions you have.

STATEMENT OF HON. BILL A. MILLER, DEPUTY ASSISTANT SECRETARY OF STATE FOR HIGH–THREAT POSTS, U.S. DEPARTMENT OF STATE, WASHINGTON, DC

Mr. MILLER. Good morning, Chairman Menendez, Ranking Member Corker, and distinguished committee members. Thank you also for your invitation to appear here today to discuss embassy security.

I, too, appreciate and share your commitment to enhanced embassy security, as evidenced by your recently introduced Chris Stevens, Sean Smith, Tyrone Woods, and Glen Doherty Embassy Security and Personnel Protection Act of 2013.

Threats and attacks against our diplomatic facilities and personnel have been a concern since the inception of embassy security, almost 100 years ago. To counter these global threats, the Office of the Chief Special Agent, the forerunner of Diplomatic Security, was formed in 1916. It was not, however, until 1985, in the aftermath of the Beirut bombings, that Diplomatic Security became a Bureau within the State Department.

The DS mandate was solidified when Congress passed the Omnibus Diplomatic Security and Antiterrorism Act of 1986. At the same time, I was preparing to leave the Marine Corps, where I had my position as a Marine Corps officer, and I wanted to continue my service to the U.S. Government. And the mission envisioned of DS was part of a team—or, demonstrated the part of a team that I particularly wanted to join.

In 1987, I became a DS special agent, and since then, I have devoted my 26-year career to fulfilling the mission of DS; that is, providing a safe and secure environment for the conduct of foreign policy.

Early in my career, I was a part of the Secretary of State's protective detail. I have also served assignments in our Washington field office as the Chief of the Security and Law Enforcement Training Division, as the Chief of Counterintelligence Investigations, and as the Director of Contingency Operations. I have managed security programs as a regional security officer, also known as an RSO, in Iraq, Pakistan, Jerusalem, the Philippines, and in Egypt.

To demonstrate the depth of my experience and that of a DS special agent, I would like to highlight a few of my accomplishments.

As an RSO, I dealt daily with the possible terrorist acts that impacted the lives of Americans, to include the kidnapping of American missionaries in the Philippines, as well as participating in the capture of Ramzi Yousef, one of the main perpetrators of the 1993 World Trade Center bombing.

When the United States returned to Iraq in 2003, I was asked to serve as the first RSO and to manage the volatile security environment as we reestablished our diplomatic presence. Most recently overseas, I was the RSO in Cairo, Egypt, during the Arab

Spring. It is an experience that informs my decisionmaking as I work to ensure adequate security resources during the ongoing transition in Egypt.

After the September 2012 attacks on our facilities in Libya, Yemen, Tunisia, and Egypt and Sudan, the Department reviewed its security posture and created my position, the Diplomatic Security Deputy Assistant Secretary of State for High-Threat Posts, also known as HTP, along with providing a staff of security professionals to support high-threat, high-risk posts. The Department assessed our diplomatic missions worldwide and weighed criteria to determine which posts are designated as high-threat, high-risk. And there are now 27 posts which fall under this designation. This designation is not a static process, and the list will be reviewed annually, at a bare minimum, and more frequently, when needed. As emergent conditions substantially change, for better or for worst, at any post worldwide, high-threat, high-risk designations will shift, and missions will be added or deleted from this category. The high-threat protection directorate that I lead oversees the security operations in these high-threat, high-risk posts around the world. We coordinate strategic and operational planning and drive innovation across the broad spectrum of DS missions and responsibilities. We continue to work closely, also, with the regional bureaus to ensure that everyone has visibility of the security threats at our posts.

As the Deputy Assistant Secretary for HTP, I am responsible for evaluating, managing, and mitigating the security threats, as well as directing resource requirements at high-threat diplomatic missions. I closely follow developments, continually assess our security posture, and take all possible steps to mitigate threats and vulnerabilities.

While the Department has created a position for high-threat, high-risk post designations, we must continue to focus on embassy security worldwide. I coordinate closely with my colleagues in Diplomatic Security throughout the Department and the interagency to ensure that the threats and risk-mitigation strategies are shared globally. As you have said, we can never truly eliminate all the risks facing our dedicated personnel working overseas who advance U.S. interests. However, as the Department has said, we place the highest priority on the security of our personnel and will continue to take the steps necessary, which, in some instances, include extraordinary measures to provide for their safety.

I would like to thank you again for the opportunity to appear before the committee today and discuss the future of our embassy security. I'm available to answer any of your questions.

[The prepared statement of Mr. Miller follows:]

PREPARED STATEMENT OF BILL MILLER

Good morning, Chairman Menendez, Ranking Member Corker, and distinguished committee members. Thank you for your invitation to appear here today to discuss embassy security. We appreciate and share your commitment to enhanced embassy security, as evidenced by the recently introduced "Chris Stevens, Sean Smith, Tyrone Woods, and Glen Doherty Embassy Security and Personnel Protection Act of 2013."

Threats and attacks against our diplomatic facilities and personnel have been a concern since the inception of embassy security almost 100 years ago. To counter these global threats, the Office of the Chief Special Agent, the forerunner of diplomatic security was formed in 1916. It was not until 1985, in the aftermath of the Beirut bombings, that Diplomatic Security (DS) became a Bureau within the State Department. The DS mandate was solidified when Congress passed the Omnibus Diplomatic Security and Antiterrorism Act of 1986. When I was preparing to leave my position as a Marine Corps officer and wanted to continue my service to the U.S. Government, the mission and vision of DS was a team that I wanted to join. In 1987, I became a DS Special Agent. Since then, I have devoted my 25-year career to fulfilling the mission of DS: providing a safe and secure environment for the conduct of foreign policy.

Early in my career, I was part of the Secretary of State's protective detail. I have also served in our Washington field office, as the Chief of Security Training, Chief of Counterintelligence Investigations, and Director of Contingency Operations. I have managed security programs as a Regional Security Officer, also known as an RSO, in Iraq, Pakistan, Jerusalem, the Philippines, and Egypt. To demonstrate the depth of my experience and that of a DS Special Agent, I would like to highlight a few of my accomplishments. As an RSO, I dealt daily with possible terrorist acts that impacted the lives of Americans, including the kidnapping of Americans in the Philippines, as well as the capture of Ramzi Yousef, one of the main perpetrators of the 1993 World Trade Center bombing. When the United States returned to Iraq in 2003, I was asked to serve as the first RSO to manage the volatile security environment as we reestablished our diplomatic presence. Most recently overseas, I was the RSO in Egypt during the Arab Spring; an experience that informs my decision-making as I work to ensure adequate security resources during the ongoing transition in Egypt.

After the September 2012 attacks on our facilities in Libya, Yemen, Tunisia, Sudan, and Egypt, the Department reviewed its security posture and created my position, the Diplomatic Security Deputy Assistant Secretary of High Threat Posts, also known as HTP, along with a staff of security professional to support high-threat, high-risk posts. The Department assessed our diplomatic missions worldwide and weighed criteria to determine which posts are designated as high-threat, high-risk—there are now 27 posts which fall under this designation. This designation is not a static process and the list will be reviewed annually, at a minimum, and more frequently as needed. As emergent conditions substantially change, for better or for worse, at any post worldwide, high-threat, high-risk designations will shift, and missions will be added or deleted from this category. The HTP Directorate I oversee will lead the security operations in these high-threat, high-risk posts around the world, coordinate strategic and operational planning, and drive innovation across the broad spectrum of DS missions and responsibilities. We continue to work closely with the Regional Bureaus to ensure that everyone has visibility of the security threats at our posts.

As the Deputy Assistant Secretary for HTP, I am responsible for evaluating, managing, and mitigating the security threats, as well as directing resource requirements at high-threat diplomatic missions. I closely follow developments, continually assess our security posture, and take all possible steps to mitigate threats and vulnerabilities. While the Department has created a position for high-threat post designations, we must continue to focus on embassy security worldwide. I coordinate closely with my colleagues in DS, the Department, and the interagency to ensure the threats and risk mitigation strategies are shared globally.

We can never truly eliminate all the risks facing our dedicated personnel working overseas to advance U.S. interests. However, as the Department has said, we place the highest priority on the security of our personnel and will continue to take steps, which in some instances includes extraordinary measures, to provide for their safety.

Thank you again for the opportunity to appear before the committee today and to discuss the future of embassy security. I am available to answer any questions you may have.

The CHAIRMAN. Well, thank you both for your testimony. And let me start the first round of questions, here.

You know, I have heard from some of my colleagues that suggest that what we need is just greater oversight at State, but we do not need any money. The question is, Can you, under the existing budget, with no additional revenues, protect, throughout the world, and particularly at high-risk posts, the lives of those who are assigned to the diplomatic corps representing us worldwide?

Mr. STARR. Senator, thank you for going right to the heart of what is really important to us, in many ways: giving us the resources to address this. Two parts to this answer.

The 2013 Continuing Resolution level of funding, plus the generosity of Congress under the increased security proposal, I believe gives us the proper level of resources that we can utilize effectively now, this year and our 2014 budget request, which essentially rolls both of those pots of money into our request, as well. I believe that that amount of money gives us the ability to move forward and do the things that we need to do.

The second part of that question is, of course, as all of us have mentioned, no, we cannot guarantee that we are going to protect every single person, because we are working in highly, highly dangerous areas, in many countries. But, that level of funding, that level of resources, combined with the types of actions that we are taking, gives us a level of confidence that we have adequate and appropriate resources to address the types of threats that we need to address.

Now, it does not mean that we are going to have equivalent levels of security across the board. We are going to prioritize where we put our resources—manpower, equipment, technical equipment, where we build the new embassies—so we will obviously have places where we have lower levels of resources.

The CHAIRMAN. Right. So, let me——

Mr. STARR. But, we will do it to the best we can, sir.

The CHAIRMAN. What I am trying to get is, is that, if I zeroed out your account in the next year's budget, what would you do?

Mr. STARR. If——

The CHAIRMAN. If I zeroed out—if you did not roll over what, as you described, the largesse of the Congress, what would you do?

Mr. STARR. We would prioritize very heavily——

The CHAIRMAN. But, you are not going to be able to secure people across the globe——

Mr. STARR. No, sir.

The CHAIRMAN [continuing]. Understanding the context of security.

Secondly, if I cut it in half, what would you do?

Mr. STARR. I think that would cause a reassessment of where we could actually put people, sir. I do not think we would be able to stay in the highest-threat locations, where the U.S. national interests are most important.

The CHAIRMAN. So, there is—so, when the ARB identified—it is number 10 of their many recommendations—identified $2.2 billion as an appropriate funding level for the Capital Security Cost-Sharing Program, which the President's FY14 budget requested this amount, it was not just a number from the sky, it was based upon an analysis of the Accountability Review Board about what your challenges are, what your needs are, and what you can realistically administer over a period of time. Is that a fair statement?

Mr. STARR. Yes, sir, that is very fair.

The CHAIRMAN. And so from a security standpoint, do you have a sense of how many new facilities are needed, particularly in high-threat, high-risk locations?

Mr. STARR. Sir, within the high-threat list of 27 countries, we have a certain amount of them that have gotten new facilities, but there still are about 15 of those facilities that we do not have the proper level of what we call "post-Inman buildings." There are other places around the world where we do not have those facilities.

Going back to about 2000, after the 1998 bombings in Dar es Salaam and Nairobi, we made a calculation, which we stand to, to this day, which is that we needed approximately 175 new facilities around the world to be brought up to the highest level of security standards. In the past 13 years, we have constructed about 80 to 90 of those facilities. From 1988 to 1992, under the Inman era, we constructed 22 of those facilities. So, we are at about the 110 mark out of 175 facilities that we would like to continue working diligently to replace and put new embassies that meet blast standards, have their proper level of standoff, as mandated by Congress, have the antiram protection, and have the level of protection that we seek for our people overseas.

The CHAIRMAN. Let me ask you, What are the factors that would require the construction of a new facility versus a security upgrade at an existing facility?

Mr. STARR. Primary factor, sir, is that, in many places around the world, we do not have facilities that have setback. We cannot retrofit many of our buildings to withstand blast or direct attack without the ability to move to a new location, acquire setback, and build a facility that meets the blast standards.

The CHAIRMAN. Now, finally, where new construction is not an option because of the inability to either secure land, find a suitable location, or for other reasons, how does the Department seek to mitigate risks at high-threat, high-risk facilities?

Mr. STARR. Many of those locations, we have withdrawn our families, we have cut down and moved our staffing levels to only the personnel that we absolutely need, we have worked closely with host governments, in many cases, and asked them to close off streets around our embassies so that we can try to maintain some setback. Many of them have done that for several years, but also look to us eventually to move our facilities so they can reopen their streets. We work closely in training our personnel and then trying to train host-country forces in antiterrorism capabilities.

It is a variety of things, sir. But, the real one, where we really are faced with facilities that do not meet our security standards, we work with the host government to try to increase our setback, put up additional barriers, and harden the facilities, and then make sure that we have only the people necessary, at the post, that we need.

The CHAIRMAN. So, to recap, money is a consideration, here, in terms of your ability to say to this committee, "We are doing as best as we can in order to secure our people across the globe."

Mr. STARR. I could not say it better, sir. Yes; absolutely.

The CHAIRMAN. All right.

And then, finally, when we look at new embassy construction, I understand it is prioritized on the basis of security. Is that a correct statement, or is that an incorrect statement?

Mr. STARR. The primary driver is security, sir. We provide a list, with the Overseas Buildings Office, of our highest priorities. Within that list, as we understand, that obtaining real estate and property deals and then building a facility are a long-range and very difficult in certain places, OBO has certain flexibility, but we have reinforced with OBO, most recently as a month and a half ago, that we want them to relook at our highest-threat posts on the high-threat list and determine whether or not we can make significant progress on them.

I can give you one example, sir. After 30 years of trying to find land for a new facility in Beirut and start the construction of a new facility, we believe we are going to be successful in the next couple of years. It looks like we have a land deal, and it looks like we are going to be able to actually replace the facility in Beirut that we have been trying to replace for many, many years.

The CHAIRMAN. Great.

And, for those of us who are not acronym proficient, OBO is?

Mr. STARR. I am sorry, sir. It is the Office of Overseas Buildings Operations.

The CHAIRMAN. All right.

Senator Corker.

Senator CORKER. Mr. Chairman, again, thank you. And thank you both for coming here.

And I know the chairman has asked, sort of, a line of questions that—which I expected that he would. And when we had the hearing—I guess, the first hearing, with the leadership that put forth the ARB, I mean, immediately they were talking about money. And it seems like whenever there is a problem, that is the first place we go. And I understand we may need to look at that.

At the same time, as we look at your plans, I know you currently have $1.4 billion, and you have asked for $800 million more. And I see that we are spending a huge amount of money on facilities at The Hague, Oslo, Port Moresby. And even in places where we have construction underway, like Beirut, the new Embassy will not be ready for another 6 years. And, at the same time—so, this is a lot of money that is being spent in places that, candidly, the security issues are not necessarily urgent, like we have in some of the places I mentioned earlier, in Pakistan and Sudan.

So, it just seems to me that, from the standpoint of the immediate security issues that our personnel has, and all of us, including you, wanting them to be safe, our priorities are not aligned with what it is we are hoping to do for our outstanding Foreign Service officers. And I just wish you would respond to that.

Mr. STARR. Sir, I appreciate the point that you are making. And, in very many ways, on an everyday basis, we are trying to address the immediate security concerns, through programs like increased training of our personnel and our officers; lessons that we learned from Benghazi, like, you know, How do we increase our fire safety awareness and how do we provide safety?—or, How do we provide countermeasures to fire as a weapon? In those places where we cannot get new facilities, we are doing security upgrades and working our host governments, to the best that we can.

But, I think it is clear that, while we are doing the immediate and short-term needs that we need to be addressing, we are also asking for the ability to address the long-term needs so that, as we move forward in the future, we put ourselves, overall, in a better position.

In 1997, our embassies in Dar es Salaam and Nairobi were essentially rated as low-threat posts. We did not know, at that point, that we were going to be seeing the phenomenon of terrorism working outside of the small Middle East number of posts that we were mostly concerned with.

Today, we know that global terrorism is exactly that: global. It is a worldwide phenomenon. We do not know where we are going to be, a decade from now. We did not foresee the Arab Spring rise. We did not really foresee, in many cases, the challenges that we would be facing through the Middle East.

So, our best answer, on a long-term basis, is, while we are addressing the short-term, immediate needs that we have to for our personnel and their safety, is also to address the long-term needs so that we put ourselves, overall, in a better position.

As I said, when we looked at our facilities from a vulnerability standpoint, back in 2000, we looked at it and said we need probably 175 new facilities. The facility in Oslo does not have any setback. It has no blast resistance. It is not bullet resistant. It provides a very low level of safety for our personnel. I hope to be able to replace even facilities in countries like that, as we go along, for the future.

Senator CORKER. Well, I mean, is the answer yes or no? Are you going to use some of this $800 million to harden and deal with some of the immediate issues? Yes or no?

Mr. STARR. Yes, sir. We are going to try to address our immediate issues and our long-term issues. But, it is a combination of both. But, certainly our immediate issues come first. We sent out combined State Department and military ISAT teams to look at our highest threat-level posts in the aftermath of Benghazi. We have dedicated an immense amount of resources to trying to upgrade even further those places that we have on our high-threat list, and continue to do that.

Senator CORKER. What about the training facility? I have received some calls from folks, other Senators about this. I understand training now takes place in facilities that are already built, though I have not visited them, personally. You can share with me your own experiences—but, why would we go ahead and—you know, at a time when we need capital to harden facilities to deal with some of the longer term needs you are talking about—why would we be expending so much money to build a new training facility, when apparently those needs are being taken care of in another existing facility?

Mr. STARR. Thank you for that question, Senator. This is a question that is very close to my heart.

We are currently using a leased facility that is, on weekends, a racetrack facility in West Virginia. We use it 5 days a week. We can train approximately 2,500 Foreign Service officers a year in what we call ''fact training,'' the types of training that—not for DS agents like Bill and myself, but for regular Foreign Service officers. We give them high-speed training in driving vehicles, antiram training. We give them training—basic firearms training on how to make weapons safe, first-aid training. We expose them to explosives so that the first time they hear a bomb going off, they can understand that, if they have survived it, what their next responsibility is—you know, deal with themselves and then deal with others and first aid. This level of fact training, we have found through the years, has definitely saved lives overseas and prepared our people to serve in the environments that we are sending them.

Regretfully, the 2,300 people that I can train per year does not come close—does not even meet the number of people that we have at our high-threat posts, alone. We have certain of our high-threat posts where we can only give our people a 4-hour online course and say, ''Please take this course.''

So, the capacity of the current facility that we are leasing in West Virginia cannot meet our training needs. Our long-term goal, given where we are putting people out overseas, is to train every single Foreign Service officer every 5 years on the types of hard-skills security training that we believe Foreign Service officers need; and, in many cases, their adult family members, as well.

So, the current facility does not meet our requirements, does not even meet our highest threat-level requirements, and is a leased facility that, at some point, may not be available to us.

So, we are seeking to put, in one place, close to where we have our partners, the Marine Corps, military, intelligence community, and the rest of the Foreign Service training apparatus—we are seeking to build a hard-skills training center where we can put 8 to 10,000 people a year through this type of training. We believe that that will give us the ability—in addition to hardening our facilities, the most important side—training our people before they go overseas.

Senator CORKER. And if I could just ask one last question. You know, we have talked at a 30,000-foot level here about capital expenditures. And I know we are going to be in much more detail between our staffs. I mean, we now have talked a little bit about training, and I understand how important that is, and we certainly plan to get into more details with you there as we move ahead.

I guess the last piece is, then, you know, you require people within the State Department to execute. And again, I know we have had a situation where the State Department has reviewed functions. We had four personnel that have been put on leave and are still being paid. And, just for what it is worth, it does feel that there is a degree of lack of accountability, to put it nicely. And I just wonder if you might address that, also. Because you build great facilities, you train well, but, if people do not execute and there is not that accountability, we still have breakdowns and people are in situations that they should not be in. So, could you address that issue for us today?

Mr. STARR. Yes, sir. Thank you for the question.

I think my first answer would be—is that Bill Miller, sitting next to me, and my coming back after 4 years at the United Nations and 29 years in Diplomatic Security, there is nobody that takes this responsibility more seriously than we do.

The people that we manage and the staffs that we have, the agents that we train, the security protective specialists, the engineers, the people that we have in Diplomatic Security are dedicated and ready to give their lives to protecting our people overseas. And I will simply say that you will not find anybody more ready to take the responsibility or make the decisions that have to be made than myself or Bill Miller or the rest of my senior staff in Diplomatic Security.

I understand that there are still questions about the four individuals. I was not here at the time. I do understand that it is complex, because there are sets of rules and procedures within the Foreign Service about disciplining people. It is my clear understanding that this entire issue is at the Secretary of State's level, that he is getting recommendations on how to deal with this, and he will, finally, make the decision on what is going to be the outcome with the four people there.

I will tell you, sir, that three of those four individuals, I know well and have worked with closely. These are people that have given their careers to Diplomatic Security, as well, and the security of the Department of State. And I have a great deal of admiration for them. It does not excuse the fact that we had a terrible tragedy in Benghazi. And I think that the Secretary and his staff will make the proper decisions on the disposition of those cases.

But, I do want to tell you that that is the same management team that was in place when our embassies were attacked in Cairo, in Tunisia, in Khartoum, all through the years that we have had multiple attacks in Yemen, in Afghanistan, and in Iraq. Those people performed admirably. And it is my hope that their entire career is not blotted by one single action, because they are, in many ways, as dedicated as we are.

But, I will tell you that Bill and I will do our absolute best, and we will bear whatever responsibility needs to be taken.

Senator CORKER. Well, listen, I thank you for that. And I just would say that, look, I do not think anybody here is on a witch hunt. And, candidly, I could not pick these four individuals out of a lineup. I do not know that I have ever even met them. I do think it is important for the culture of the State Department and, candidly, for the U.S. Government in general, that either, you know, it be stated that these people made mistakes that should not have been made and are held accountable, or not. And again, whatever is the right decision, I think we will all be there. But, this sort of vague place that we are in probably needs to end soon.

And again, I thank you for your response, and I hope the Secretary of State will deal with this quickly, because it has been a long time. But, I thank you, and I look forward to working with you and the chairman as we move ahead.

The CHAIRMAN. Well, thank you, Senator Corker.

Because this is—I take this obligation very seriously. At least on my watch, to the extent that I can, I am not going to have anybody exposed and at risk as a result of inaction by this committee. So, I am going to, at times here, engage in a followup so that we have a sequential record that makes the facts. There are two things that Senator Corker said and you responded to that I want to get a little clarity, so I will hope my colleagues will indulge me as I move to them next.

He asked you a very good question—you know, immediate needs versus long-term needs. And you responded that you are working on immediate needs. Of course, ''immediate needs'' means to the extent that you can mitigate what exists at a post, because if you do not have a setback, you are not going to be able to mitigate that fully until you have a new site and a new construction. If you do not have a setback, and you are talking about hardening—OK, fine, but hardening without a setback has limited capabilities.

So, when you say, in the balance between what some may view as the long term, which you described as, hopefully, getting to a point in which all of our locations are as best protected under the threats that we could envision today, regardless of where they are located in the world, because we do not know where the next high-risk posts will be, where the movement of a terrorist activity will take place, and then we will all regret that, well, we did not think that an Oslo meant that much, by way of example. So, when you say you are mitigating, you are mitigating—correct me if I am wrong, here, and I would like the record to reflect whatever it is that—what are you mitigating in the short term—what are you capable of mitigating in the short term if you have an embassy or other site that is not fully living to the specifications of what you and the Congress have devised as what is a secure location?

Mr. STARR. Mr. Chairman, what we can mitigate in those locations is, first, a function of what our analysis, in terms of the threat and the overall situation in the country, tells us. In a place like Oslo today, we have a full-functioning staff and a fully functioning embassy, despite the fact that we do not have a setback or a secure facility. The reason we can do that is that we have excellent cooperation from the host government, we do not have information that indicates to us that we are running a tremendously high risk by leaving them in this facility for the time being, and we have national security imperatives that we are carrying out, Foreign Service officers working on different things every single day.

But, to give you another example, sir, is—in Cairo today—and Cairo is a—not an Inman building; it is a pre-Inman building, but quite a robust facility—when the situation changed dramatically in Cairo, when we saw specific threats, when we saw the social upheaval happening on the ground—in the last several weeks, we have evacuated what we call ''ordered departure.'' We have moved out all of our families and we have moved out all nonessential personnel, nonemergency personnel. And these are the types of things that we can do to mitigate threats, where we do not have a facility that necessarily meets, you know, the highest level of standards.

There are things that we can do, in terms of, as I say, asking the host government to block off streets for us, if they will cooperate——

The CHAIRMAN. I gather that. I do not want to cut you short, but——

Mr. STARR. Yes.

The CHAIRMAN [continuing]. What I am trying to get to is Senator Corker's concern—or at least it seems to me his concern, as expressed at various times now, and today as well—between the immediate and the long term. To the extent—Is this a fair statement? To the extent that you can mitigate something in the immediate term, you are seeking to do that. Is that a fair statement?

Mr. STARR. Absolutely, sir.

The CHAIRMAN. Now, that does not mean that mitigation of the immediate is the desired goal, because, in fact, you may not be able to mitigate beyond—if you do not have a setback, if you do not have a hardened facility, if you do not have all the other elements that are in play for what we consider a fully secured facility. Is that a fair statement?

Mr. STARR. Exactly. Yes, sir.

The CHAIRMAN. All right. Now, that gives us a little balance as to what the immediate versus the long term means.

With reference to the question of employees, I agree. I agree in accountability, and I agree in performance. Now, I read the ARB's recommendation, number 23, which said that, ''The Board is of the view that findings of unsatisfactory leadership performance by senior officials in relation to the security incident under review should be a potential basis for discipline recommendations by future Accountability Boards, and would recommend a revision of Department regulations or amendment to the relevant statute to this end.'' In essence, when they were here, as well, and testified to this question, they said, ''Under the existing statutory authority, there are limitations.'' What is the proof point that you have to have in order to discipline somebody?

So, I do not know if you have had the opportunity to look at section 203 of the legislation that I have promoted, S. 980, that I believe satisfied the ARB's recommendation in that regard, which would then give the Secretary the authority to fire individuals who have exhibited unsatisfactory leadership in relation to a security incident. Do you believe that that section would give the Secretary that ability?

Mr. STARR. Yes, sir, I do. I believe it is important to give that additional flexibility, and I think that helps us.

The CHAIRMAN. Thank you very much.

Senator Cardin, thank you for your forbearance.

Senator CARDIN. Well, thank you, Mr. Chairman. Let me just concur with your observation.

Our committee has a very important responsibility for oversight. And I appreciate the two witnesses that are here. It is our responsibility to review the steps that you have taken and resources that you have. But, we also have a responsibility to make sure that tools are available for embassy security. And that is a responsibility of the entire Senate. The Appropriations Committee has the responsibility on the resources. This committee has the responsibility as to whether the policies are right. And I just want to applaud the chairman for S. 980. I think that gives us a way to make sure that you have the adequate tools in order to manage the security of our embassies. And the chairman's followup questions, I think, underscored some of those issues, and I thank you very much, Mr. Chairman, for your leadership on this issue, but also recognizing the dual responsibility we have on oversight and to make sure that the tools and resources are available.

I want to follow up on facilities, because I have had a chance to visit many of our embassies. And there is a common theme, except for the very new embassies, when you are able to talk frankly with the embassy personnel, there is always concerns about the facilities, that they could be better. And I know that you did a review and a list was compiled several years ago, and I know that we have also made progress. And I expect that this list is updated by circumstances in country, et cetera. But, is it time for us to do another evaluation, globally, of our facilities, recognizing that circumstances have changed?

I, personally, believe we need to do a better job. Oslo is an important ally, a friend. I have been to that embassy. I understand that it is not a high-risk area, but they should have adequate facilities, based upon the security needs and efficiency factors. And, in many embassies around the world, the United States does not have the combination of space, efficiency, and security that is ideal for us to carry out our mission.

Mr. STARR. Sir, I believe that is an accurate statement. It is, in many cases, more than just security, but certainly security is our overriding factor at this point. But, I believe you are accurate when you say that, in many cases, we do not have either the space or the types of facilities that we need.

That is why, when we build new facilities, the primary thing that we are trying to achieve is security, but the Office of Overseas Buildings looks clearly at what our staffing levels need to be, where we are going to be in the future, what types of operational and functional space we need; and that includes things like much larger consular operations, in many places. We have many other agencies in our embassies, as well. And that is all wrapped into what it is that we are doing and how we build buildings and where we build buildings.

So, sir, I could not agree with you more. It is a combination of factors. But, we believe we still need probably at least another 75 or so major buildings.

Senator CARDIN. Mr. Chairman, I would urge that we look at a way in that we can get an updated realistic inventory of what we need, globally, to meet the challenges.

I really do applaud former Secretary Clinton and President Obama for recognizing the important role that our diplomatic missions play in our national security. They need to have the resources in order to be able to carry that out in a safe manner, in an efficient manner. And I just think we could use a better blueprint than the one that was developed 5 or 6 or 7 years ago.

Mr. STARR. Senator Cardin, I will take that back, and I am sure the Office of Overseas Buildings Operations, and probably with us, would be willing to come up and work with any of your staff and give you the information that you would like.

Senator CARDIN. I appreciate that.

Let me move on to a second issue on security, and that is the confidence and support that we have from the local government and authorities. I know that it varies by country. And that is evaluated as part of the security mission that you have to undertake.

Can you just briefly outline how the confidence we have in the local government's ability to respond or to work with us on security issues, factors into the equation on our security needs?

I wanted to give Mr. Starr a break. So, Mr. Miller, if you could respond that, that would be good.

Mr. MILLER. I appreciate that, sir. I was beginning to feel a little left out. [Laughter.]

If I could go back a moment to the ISAT teams that went out in November, I led one of those teams as we went about assessing our various missions, the 19 missions that we very quickly assessed and felt that were our most vulnerable at that time. One of the things, one of the legs that we were assessing was our host nation's willingness and capability to defend the mission in accordance with their Vienna requirements. As we look at that, we have to roll that into "If it's weak on one leg, we have to strengthen the other." And that would be our ability to withstand an attack, say, for instance, as we did for quite some time in Khartoum and in Tunisia, about 8 hours as those facilities were attacked in early September, as well.

So, if we have a weakness on one side, we have to be able to mitigate that by strengthening on another. It is not always possible, however. And that calls into play, then, a greater requirement for our diplomatic cadre to work with the host-nation political counterparts to ensure that they live up to their responsibilities, just as we do here for them in the United States.

It is something that we try to address, where we can, with training, through our antiterrorism assistance programs and other bilateral training programs that the U.S. Government provides to help bolster their own professional capabilities and, hopefully, build it up to the point where we can trust, as we do in most places, their ability to secure us.

Senator CARDIN. I would just make one observation. I would hope that we engage the political apparatus of our country at the highest levels if we need more cooperation from host countries.

I want to ask one more question on one of the ARB recommendations to address language capacity. Could you just briefly update us as to how that recommendation is being implemented?

Mr. MILLER. Certainly. And as this applies primarily to the capacity for Arabic language skills, the Foreign Service Institute has been working very diligently with the rest of the Department, to include with Diplomatic Security, to assess what our language requirements are for our special agents as they engage with their host-nation counterparts.

We anticipate, I believe, that the first class begins this next month, or early September, to give those skills, or the opportunity to acquire the skills for our special agents in such a way that they will be able to work in an emergency situation. Realizing that it is a long-term process to acquire proficiency that allows them to converse proficiently, that process can be upward of 2 years for someone like myself, shorter for those who are a little brighter. But, it is a very difficult process. We are hoping to achieve that with a short-term objective with our immediate security language course in Arabic.

Senator CARDIN. Thank you.

Thank you, Mr. Chairman.

The CHAIRMAN. Well, thank you, Senator Cardin.

And, Mr. Miller, feel free to join in on any answers that you want. We want a full record, as much as possible, so do not hesitate to jump in.

Senator Flake.

Senator FLAKE. Thank you. And I apologize for not being here. And I apologize if this has been asked and answered probably three times by now with regard to the legislation that has been introduced.

Assuming that legislation were in place and implemented, would it have affected the outcome in Benghazi, simply because it was not an embassy or even a consulate? Would it have made a difference there or—in your opinion?

Mr. Starr.

Mr. STARR. Benghazi was at a threat level that we should have reprioritized what we were doing within our existing capabilities. I thank the chairman for introducing this legislation. In the long term, it will help us on a number of different fronts. But, I am not going to sit here and tell you that the tragedy in Benghazi could have been avoided, had we had this legislation. I think that was a question that we did not understand the situation that we were in, and perhaps we should have had more resources or we should have made a decision to evacuate that post earlier.

But, you know, we very much appreciate this legislation. It will help us in many, many ways. It will strengthen our capability to stay in places where the threats are greater. But, I am not going to blame Benghazi on the lack of this legislation.

Senator FLAKE. Do you have anything to add?

Mr. MILLER. No, sir.

Senator FLAKE. OK.

Benghazi was a particular situation there, given the makeup of the government and the situation just to—you know, the newness of all this. What lessons have we learned from that, that can be applied elsewhere, in terms of our relationship with a host nation? The host nation did not even know this facility was there, I understand, or they were not informed of it. What protocols have we put in place, if any, after that, to make sure we have better cooperation with the host nation, in terms of security needs?

Mr. MILLER. One of the chief issues, I think, that we have realized, and was addressed in the ARB, was the fact that all of our facilities should meet OSPB standards—Overseas Security Policy Board standards—for physical security. In this instance—and I was not in a position to know why—but, in this instance, they were not met. There were no waivers that were granted. That has been rectified. We will not have a temporary facility that has not been signed off on at the highest levels, wherein a balance of our national security interests and the diplomatic imperatives are weighed against the security threat. So, I would say that is one positive outcome of the ARB.

Senator FLAKE. Thank you, Mr. Chairman.

The CHAIRMAN. Thank you, Senator Flake.

Senator Kaine.

Senator KAINE. Thank you, Mr. Chair.

And, to our witnesses, I appreciate you being here today.

My first hearing as a Senator was the hearing with Secretary Clinton to talk about the Benghazi incident and the ARB recommendations, and it was a very memorable one; I will never forget that first hearing. I reviewed the ARB in advance of the hearing, to prepare—and, Mr. Chair, I imagine you know this—there are so many recommendations that you kind of personally fix upon a couple, and there are a couple that I was particularly interested in.

One was the recommendation about the expansion of the Marine Security Guard program. And the second was the recommendation about training of our State Department personnel.

In the packet of materials that we were given for this hearing, there is a New York Times graphic, where there is a summary, as of May 20, how far along we are in meeting the ARB recommendations. And there is sort of a spectrum in each of these various recommendations, from, basically, "not started" to "completed." And in each of the recommendations, there is sort of a New York Times assessment of where we are.

The Marine Security Guard one is sort of lower than the midpoint, but the lowest one, the one that is most near "not even started yet," is the recommendation about: to improve the training of employees headed to high-threat posts and expand the number of posts where additional security training is required.

Assistant Secretary Starr, you talked about the issue, in response to questioning from Senator Corker, about the need for the training facility for State Department employees. And you and I have met about this previously. And the chairman's proposed legislation addresses this. But, just to give some history for everyone here, the State Department began trying to find a training facility to replace the racetrack, that was used during the week, about 4 years ago. They began this long before Benghazi, long before the ARB. And there has been a 4-year effort that considered 80 different sites for this training facility, and it eventually dwindled down, whittled down—some communities did not want it—and with the particular requirements, largely to involve a facility that would be close to partners, synergy with the Marine Security Guard and others, it dwindled down and there was a preference for expanding this program at a Guard base—a National Guard base in Virginia, Fort Pickett. And that was, basically, the preference that we were moving toward before Benghazi and before the ARB.

After the incident at Benghazi, the ARB report has a recommendation, recommendation number 17, that specifically focuses upon the need to move out of this rented facility and find a permanent facility for embassy training.

In February, just a few months ago, the State Department communicated to Congress and indicated that they were about to issue an EIS for Fort Pickett, but, in April, there was another letter that suggested this was now delayed, largely because of an inquiry from the OMB about whether or not we could maybe do this kind of a half version or a knockoff version at some other facility. And I gather that there has been some exploration of an existing facility in Georgia that would not have the synergies with the Marine Security Guard Program, that would not have synergies with the other intelligence agencies with whom our Department of State staff worked.

So, it appears that this process that was moving forward before Benghazi and before the ARB to actually require this training capacity is now, after Benghazi and after the ARB, being thrown into kind of a question-mark status.

It would be ironic—that is the wrong word. It would be tragic if a process that was moving toward better training, optimizing training for Secretary of State—or Department of State staff before Benghazi and before the ARB, would be now slowed down, watered down, diluted after we know what we know as a result of those horrible incidents on September 11, 2013.

And so, Secretary Starr and Mr. Miller, what I would like to ask—Assistant Secretary Starr—what I would like to ask you is, From the State Department's standpoint, is it still your professional belief that the site that was identified by the Department of State at Fort Pickett is the most consistent with both the desire to increase training and also most consistent with the ARB recommendation that was forwarded to Congress by the committee?

Mr. STARR. Senator Kaine, thank you for your question. The answer is simple: yes, sir. We still believe that the site that we chose at Fort Pickett gives us the best ability to train the numbers of personnel that we need to train; to incorporate our partners in the various other U.S. Government agencies, that are critical to our training, into that training; to build the synergies that we have with our own Foreign Service Institute and our own training regimens up here. Yes, sir, we still believe that is the best answer.

Senator KAINE. Mr. Miller, from your standpoint?

Mr. MILLER. I can only echo what Assistant Secretary Staff said. We have to have the synergy in order to develop the relationships with our training partners as well as for the students who are going through. And we both could give you numerous examples of opportunities that foreign affairs officers have had to participate in actual lifesaving events, where they have benefited from the training that they had at the racetrack, which has so well served us throughout my career. But, we can do better. And if we can do better, we absolutely have to, because we are talking about people's lives.

Senator KAINE. Thank you. I do not have any other questions.

Senator CARDIN [presiding]. Senator Barrasso.

Senator BARRASSO. Thank you, Mr. Chairman.

You know, the security of brave men and women serving our Nation overseas is critically important. To me, the Accountability Review Board made it clear that the State Department did not give the mission in Benghazi the personnel and resources needed to ensure their security. So, I just wanted to make sure that we are learning from those failures and implementing real reforms.

With regard to risk mitigation, I understand that we must accept a certain amount of risk to operate in areas like Benghazi. The Accountability Review Board stated, "Risk mitigation involved two imperatives: engagement and security, which require wise leadership, good intelligence and evaluation, proper defense, and strong preparedness, and, at times, downsizing indirect access,'' they say, "and even withdrawal."

So, the question: What are the factors that the Department of State considers when determining whether a location is simply too dangerous to support a diplomatic presence?

Mr. Miller.

Mr. MILLER. Thank you, Senator.

We look at three basic questions: the host nation's capability and willingness, as I said earlier. We look at the current threat streams, those threats which have developed, that we are aware of, that direct themselves to our facilities. And then, we also look at the physical presence that we are able to maintain, based on our physical security posture at post. And, as we balance those three and any possible mitigation, we then move forward with our diplomatic engagement. If we cannot balance those three, then we have to assess those options which you have just addressed.

Senator BARRASSO. Are there posts, currently, that you have identified as needing to either be downsized or closed?

Mr. MILLER. I can point back to Bangui, which we evacuated late last fall—late December. We are constantly evaluating other posts. A good example is our U.S. Embassy in Cairo, over the past month, as they have gone through the large disturbances, not only in Cairo, but throughout the country. So, it is a constant evaluative process that we go through and assess, then, what our next steps may possibly be.

Senator BARRASSO. Could I ask about the Inspector General's audit of June 30, came out—2013—released its audit of compliance with physical and procedural security standards at select high-threat-level posts. And I am concerned that it has been 10 months since the terrorist attacks in Benghazi, yet the Inspector General found that there are high-threat-level posts are failing to comply with security standards. I do not know if you have seen the audit yet. Can you explain to the committee why these problems are happening, and what the plan and timeline is for, you know, remedying these issues?

Mr. MILLER. Thank you. I think it is important that we do point out some differences that we may have with the Office of Inspector General when they do provide a report, as this one. I think it is important to note that the high-threat, high-risk posts that I am responsible for leading and supervising the management of their programs, I do not believe they visited any of those posts. When they are referring to high-threat, that is a very often-used and not-well-defined term. So, as they look at the various recommendations, it should be parsed very carefully when we look at the HTP posts for which I am responsible.

I will say that we are continuing to work with the OIG to address their concerns. We want to ensure that our people do have the best-possible protection, and we value the OIG's perspective. But, I know DS, or Diplomatic Security, is working with the OIG to find common ground.

Senator BARRASSO. Well, thank you for that clarification.

Thank you, Mr. Chairman.

Senator CARDIN. Thank you.

Let me thank both of our witnesses, not just for your testimony, but for the incredible service that you are providing our country. It is an extremely difficult time, and obviously the safety of our personnel is an important responsibility. So, we thank you very much.

We also appreciate your willingness to work with this committee. There has been a lot of questions asked that I think will involve us working together to make sure that we have safe facilities and personnel in the right place, et cetera.

As I said earlier, we have a responsibility, not only of oversight, but to be your partners, and we look forward to working with you to protect the dedicated men and women who serve our Nation in foreign posts around the world.

With that, the committee will stand adjourned.

[Recess.]

The CHAIRMAN [presiding]. The committee will come to order. I apologize for the confusion.

I understand that facility training had a indepth discussion, I assume. Is that correct? So, let me ask, if I may, a couple of questions, just to conclude, then.

One is, I want to go back to the questions that Senator Flake raised with you. And, for my purpose, they are not Benghazi-specific, but they are about temporary and mixed-use facilities. My understanding is that the U.S. Special Mission in Benghazi was a temporary facility, and that the Overseas Security Policy Board standards for facilities apply to all facilities, including temporary facilities.

In a report that the ARB issued, the State Department noted that it would reissue this long-established policy to all posts by January of this year. Do we know, was that policy reissued?

Mr. MILLER. It was reissued. I believe it was January the 23rd.

The CHAIRMAN. OK. And how are the Overseas Security Policy Board standards enforced at temporary facilities?

Mr. STARR. Sir, when we move back into a country—and this is really where we are going to experience temporary facilities—one of the things that we are going to have to do is determine what our presence is going to be, and then we are going to have to determine what facilities are available and whether or not we can balance the need versus the safety.

Part of the process is looking closely at what facilities are available, what it will cost to do those facilities, and whether or not we have the ability to do it.

We are currently not in Somalia. We send temporary-duty personnel into Somalia because we do not have a facility that we think could meet our requirements at the moment. And I think that, perhaps, is the best judgment I can give you.

We are very vocal and very clear when we think that we do not have an answer that can meet the security requirements.

We are very concerned about places like Goma. We only allow temporary-duty travel in, working very closely with the United Nations. We do not have a facility that meets our needs there at the moment.

Should the Department make a determination that we need to go back into those places, we use the integrated planning cells to determine what we need to have. We have to make a determination whether we have the internal resources to meet those needs or have to come to Congress for a supplemental to do it. We have developed certain new tools to help us.

One of the things we learned out of Iraq, when we had many, many people in trailers in many places, and then we would take these trailers and we would put sandbags around them, and then we would put overhead cover, and then we would put walls around them—we have developed something called ''a hardened-alternative trailer system,'' which is a highly blast-resistant, bulletproof trailer, at this point, that provides a high degree of overhead protection built right in. So, we are trying to develop new tools that will give us reasonably safe and secure accommodations, and even offices, in these temporary-type situations.

The CHAIRMAN. So, let me go to part B of this particular Benghazi-type set of circumstances. And that is: In instances where a facility is shared or is used principally by a U.S. Government agency other than the Department of State, how does the interagency process address security needs at that facility? Who takes the lead?

Mr. STARR. The individual agency will be responsible for upgrading the facility, but it still is upgrading to the OSPB, the Overseas Security Policy Board, standards. And if they do not meet the standards, they go through the same waiver and exception processes.

The CHAIRMAN. Very good.

Now, I want, for the records purposes, to establish something that I think we, on the committee, know—you, certainly, in the Department, know—but I do not think the general public knows. And that is the Marine Guard attachment to embassies. Until now—correct me if I am wrong—the Marine Guard attachments to embassies was, in essence, for the security of sensitive and classified documents. Is that correct?

Mr. STARR. That is essentially correct, sir. The staffing levels of marines that we were putting in facilities was essentially to meet that requirement: 24-hour protection for classified assets and operations and information.

The CHAIRMAN. Now, most people see the Marine Guards—I think even Members of Congress, when they visited abroad—and thought that somehow they were about protecting the embassy, its personnel, and whatever else, including documents, was in there. But, that really was not the core focus. Their core focus, up until a new recent agreement, was to give the time, should an embassy be overrun, for the purposes of being able to deal with classified documents. Is that a fair statement?

Mr. STARR. That is correct, sir.

The CHAIRMAN. All right. Now, I understand that, at least at high-threat posts, there is an additional mandate or responsibility that we have asked the Marines to perform. Is that correct?

Mr. STARR. Yes, sir.

The CHAIRMAN. And what would that be?

Mr. STARR. We have renegotiated the Memorandum of Agreement with the Marine Corps between the Department of State and clearly emphasized that our new mandate is equal protection for our personnel and our facilities in our embassies while protecting classified information.

Sir, if I may——

The CHAIRMAN. Yes.

Mr. STARR. Even when we had our smaller numbers assigned to our detachments, in many cases, you know, six or seven marines, and the primary responsibility was protection of classified information, there was not a marine out there, and there was not an RSO out there, that did not understand that, in extremis, their job was to protect the people. But, we were not staffing with enough marines, necessarily, to take on that role. And what we are working with the Marine Corps is in—particularly in our high-threat locations, to increase the numbers of marines at each one of these posts so that they are better capable of doing the defense portion, as well.

The CHAIRMAN. I appreciate you expounding upon that, because I did not suggest to mean that marines would stand by and see people killed. But, certainly there was no staffing level to be able to accomplish that, particularly at high-threat posts.

Is the new Marine understanding that has come together with the State Department on high-threat posts or globally?

Mr. STARR. The Memorandum of Agreement is global. The reality is that we are concentrating on our highest-threat-level posts and increasing our marine staffing at those locations.

The CHAIRMAN. OK.

And then, finally, I want to get to host-government capacity. The Accountability Review Board found that the Libyan Government's response to be profoundly lacking on the night of the attacks. A host government's support posture relies on both the host government's capacity as well as their will. Those are two—critically important. You can have the will but not have the capacity; you can have the capacity but not have the will. They both need to be there.

So, as we look beyond Libya—and we are looking, now, globally—how do you assess these variables? How do you quantify them? How do these determinations go into your overall security assessment? And is the provision that we have included in the legislation which deals with the question, not of the lowest cost, but the best cost for performance, as well, to give you the flexibility, particularly in places where that will be critical to security, a desired flexibility?

I know there are multiple questions in there, so——

Mr. STARR. let me take the last part of it and then turn to Bill on part of this.

On the contracting, sir, we believe that it is critical. And we thank you very much for recognizing that the situations in almost all of our posts are different. And, in certain cases, where we do not have, perhaps, the level of support, because of willingness or capability, from the host government, situations may arise where the idea of lowest-cost technically acceptable contracting is not going to give us the guard force that we think that we could get if we had another instrument to contract with.

So, we want to thank you. We do believe that adding this capability, not just at our high-threat posts, but where we believe there is a clear indication that this will increase significantly our security capabilities, it gives us a tool to do that, sir.

So, yes, I think it is an important step that allows us to address some of the inherent capabilities when we do not necessarily have the level of support from our host government that we would like.

On the specific——

The CHAIRMAN. How about the questions of, How do you assess the host-government's ability, willingness? How do you quantify it? How do you make those determinations to factor in your overall security assessing?

Mr. MILLER. To some extent, it is a subjective call. But, we quantify it, as much as we possibly can, through our various partners with us at the embassy who help to assess the training that the host services have received. Historically, in many posts, we have a relationship that has gone back for a number of decades, and we can quantify, then, what our expectation should be and how well they can live up to those expectations.

In some instances, because of recent instability, that expectation has been nullified. And then it is a matter of us taking the opportunity, as I said in my opening statement, to go to extraordinary measures, above those measures which are standard. And, in those instances of—the best-value contracting gives us the opportunity to achieve a level of competence with our local guard forces that we would not necessarily be able to achieve with the host-nation services.

Mr. STARR. Mr. Chairman, if I may, I think we can quantify the capabilities pretty well by working closely with our Defense colleagues or intelligence colleagues, our own security staff. We can see pretty well, and make a pretty good determination of, the capabilities of the host government.

Much more subjective is this question of what is the particular willingness at a time. And we are much more sensitive, the entire Department is, to having a better analysis capability and having our political officers and our ambassadors really weighing in on what is the particular host-government desire to help us in a particular time.

There are certain places where we could have a great deal of willingness on a Tuesday afternoon, and, in some cases, by Friday afternoon it may not be there. And this is, I think, part of the dilemma, but it is also part of our solution, which is for our security personnel, Bill and I and others, to work much more closely with our regional bureaus and with our ambassadors.

The CHAIRMAN. I have one final question, and that is on the question of intelligence and its use, integration into your analysis, and to looking at changing events, which might indicate a different threat level, that we may not have traditionally thought of as necessarily looking at a different threat level. In the new paradigm in which we live in, which, unfortunately, requires us to think outside of the box, you know, the terrorists have to get only lucky once; we have to get it right 100 percent of the time. That is a tough challenge, but that is our challenge.

How are you integrating the use of intelligence? Are you receiving the flow of information that is essential, I would think, for you to continue to make an analysis on an in-real-time ongoing basis so that you can adjust accordingly where you need to?

Mr. STARR. Yes, sir. The relationship across the spectrum of intelligence community and us has broadened and deepened. We have officers that—from other agencies—that are working with us at our desks, in our offices, now. The level of coordination that goes on, in terms of discussion of threats, is deeper and wider, and held both at the working level and at the national security staff level. The coordination that we have with our regional bureaus now— every weekday morning, and Saturdays and Sundays as necessary, we start off looking at the threats that have come in most recently. In those same meetings, we have representatives from the regional bureaus of the Department of State so that we are linking up the political with the intelligence that is coming in.

If I can say one thing, sir, that—one major strategic lesson that came out of Benghazi. One of the observations of the ARB was that there was no specific intelligence in Benghazi to indicate that there was a threat—going to be a threat that night. And I think it—you can lull yourself into a position, where, if there is no specific intelligence, you say, "OK, we must be OK." I think one of the major changes that has happened is that we are much more aware of the larger atmospherics in these countries—the political, the social, what is going on in terms of Web activity, social networking—trying to keep abreast of what we see is going on in that country, in addition to whether or not we have specific intelligence threats, is a much deeper, much broader effort than we have had before, as well.

So, I think it is really both sides. It is the intelligence side that is deeper, broader, and more important to us, but it is also keeping much more abreast of what is really happening in that location, and melding the two into our decisionmaking, and then what we do as recommendations further up in the Department.

The CHAIRMAN. And when you say that your use or access or universe of intelligence is deeper and wider, are you referring to that deeper and wider as post-Benghazi?

Mr. STARR. Yes, sir.

The CHAIRMAN. Yes.

All right. With that, and seeing no other members before the committee, with the thanks of the committee both for your service and for the men and women who serve under you in protecting our diplomats abroad, you have the thanks of the committee. We look forward to a continuing engagement with you as we try to move this legislation forward.

The record will remain open until the close of business tomorrow.

And, with that, the hearing now is truly adjourned.

[Whereupon, at 11:30 a.m., the hearing was adjourned.]

ADDITIONAL MATERIAL SUBMITTED FOR THE RECORD

RESPONSES OF PRINCIPAL DEPUTY ASSISTANT SECRETARY GREGORY STARR TO
QUESTIONS SUBMITTED BY SENATOR BOB CORKER

LONG-TERM EMBASSY CONSTRUCTION VERSUS IMMEDIATE THREAT MITIGATION

The Department is requesting and S. 980 would authorize an $800 million increase from the $1.4 billion we currently spend on new embassy construction in the Capital Security Cost Sharing Program (CSCSP). In his testimony, Acting Assistant Secretary for Diplomatic Security, Gregory Starr, informed the committee that this increase would be spent on addressing immediate security deficiencies at existing posts that are not able to initiate new construction. Yet in May, committee staff were briefed about the 2013 and 2014 build plans to spend the total $2.2 billion for embassy construction, and State indicated plans to use the entire funding for long-term, new construction projects such as new embassy and consulate construction, Marine Security Guard quarters, and land acquisition.

Question A. Since S. 980 authorizes $2.2 billion for CSCP, which is used to fund new construction projects, what specific amount from this fund would be used for immediate threat mitigation in high-risk, high-threat posts that are not currently under construction for more secure facilities and how is that reflected in the 2013 and 2014 build plans that were provided to the committee?

Answer. There are 27 posts designated as High-Threat High-Risk. The Bureau of Overseas Buildings Operations (OBO) has either completed or has under construction new, secure facility projects at 12 of these posts.

Further, the Department's FY 2013 plan includes $462 million for design and construction of new Embassy compounds at three posts (N'Djamena, Nouakchott, and Beirut) designated as High-Threat High-Risk.

Site searches for the remaining 11 posts designated as High-Threat High-Risk are underway, but without a site, construction cannot be scheduled for a specific fiscal year and it would be premature to allocate funding. Once sites are acquired at any of those locations, the capital project schedule can be revised to include construction award at those posts as soon as possible.

Until sites can be acquired and new projects are underway, the Department will take steps to increase the physical security at these posts. As described in the response to question B, funding for this type of immediate security upgrade comes from outside the Capital Security Cost Sharing program. For example, a $34 million project in Tripoli funded from Embassy Security, Construction, and Maintenance Overseas Contingency Operations (ESCM/OCO) and other agency contributions is underway to include a perimeter wall, compound access control facilities, compound emergency sanctuaries, and other security enhancements recommended by the State-Department of Defense (DOD) Interagency Security Assessment Team (ISAT).

Additionally, OBO has also obligated $26 million of FY 2013 ESCM/OCO funding to implement immediate security upgrades at 19 posts (13 of which are designated as High-Threat High-Risk) in response to the recommendations of the ISAT.

Question B. If funding for immediate threat and security mitigation for U.S. personnel serving at unsecure posts that are not eligible or able to initiate new construction for safer facilities does not come from the CSCP account, what account does such funding come from and how much money is specifically allocated to such immediate threat mitigation in FY 2013 and 2014?

Answer. The Department has several options to mitigate security concerns at posts that are not immediately scheduled to receive Capital Security funding for the construction of new facilities.

Overseas Buildings Operations (OBO) Funding Options:

First and foremost is the Compound Security Program which provides physical security upgrades to existing facilities. These upgrades include perimeter walls, compound access control facilities, vehicle barriers, mantraps, compound emergency sanctuaries, and forced-entry/ballistic-resistant doors and windows. Our plan for the FY 2013 Embassy Security, Construction, and Maintenance (ESCM) appropriation includes $85.3 million for the Compound Security Program and the FY14 budget request includes $101 million. Since the inception of the Compound Security program in 1999, Congress has provided nearly $2 billion, allowing the Department to undertake security upgrades and enhancements at many posts worldwide.

In addition to the Compound Security Program, security enhancements may be incorporated into larger renovation projects that are funded from OBO's Maintenance Cost Sharing (MCS) and Major Rehabilitation Programs. The FY 2013 appropriation provides an overall program level of $270 million for MCS program, which is cost-shared between the Department ($156 million from the ESCM appropriation) and other agency contributions ($114 million) to support maintenance requirements at functional facilities occupied by multiple agencies. In FY 2013, the Major Rehabilitation Program provides $35.3 million from the ESCM appropriation for State-only functional and all residential facilities. The Department's FY 2014 budget request includes $35 million for the Major Rehabilitation Program and $130 million for the Department's share of the MCS program, which totals $167 million with other agency contributions.

Construction of new facilities that is driven by factors other than security, and is therefore not eligible for Capital Security funding, is funded from the Strategic Capital program with the ESCM account. While security vulnerability is not the reason for undertaking these projects, all facilities will be constructed to the Department's security standards. Our plan for the FY 2013 ESCM appropriation includes $69.9 million in Strategic Capital to fund the Department's share of the second phase of the new NATO headquarters facility in Brussels. There is no Strategic Capital funding in the FY 2014 budget request.

The Department also has the authority to retain the proceeds from the sale of excess and underutilized properties and use them to purchase or construct new facilities. New Embassy facilities in Berlin and Luanda were funded from proceeds of sale, as is the new London Embassy project.

Diplomatic Security (DS) Funding Options:

In FY 2013, the Department, through the Bureau of Diplomatic Security, has allocated $27.3 million of FY 2013 funds for Worldwide Security Protection (WSP) within the Diplomatic and Consular Programs (D&CP) account for physical security upgrades to mitigate security vulnerabilities at certain high-threat high-risk posts.

In addition to the $27.3 million of funds available for high-threat, high-risk physical security upgrades, $177.5 million of "undistributed" D&CP/WSP funds are available to meet emerging security needs as they arise, for a total of up to $204.8 million as needed to mitigate physical security concerns outside of CSCS.

In FY 2014, if fully funded, the President's request would provide funds within the D&CP/WSP account to mitigate physical security concerns on an as-needed basis.

Question. What actions is Diplomatic Security taking to monitor requests from overseas posts seeking security exceptions and waivers and to ensure that such exceptions and waivers are only granted where absolutely essential? Who is the most senior Department officer that is required to authorize security exceptions and waivers for high-threat posts?

Answer. The Secure Embassy Construction and Counterterrorism Act of 1999 (SECCA) requires that all newly constructed/occupied overseas U.S. diplomatic facilities possess a 100-foot setback from their perimeter, and that all U.S. Government operations be collocated on one chancery or consulate compound. Any deviation from these SECCA provisions requires a waiver from either the Secretary (all newly constructed chancery and consulate buildings that do not meet SECCA requirements) or the Assistant Secretary of Diplomatic Security (all other requests).

In addition to SECCA's requirements for colocation and setback, security standards are established by the Overseas Security Policy Board (OSPB), an intergovernmental board comprised of representatives from all agencies that operate in an overseas environment under Chief of Mission authority. The Board is chaired by the Department of State's Bureau of Diplomatic Security. OSPB physical security standards include standards for doors, perimeter walls, compound access controls, etc.

The Department strives to meet as many OSPB security standards as we can in all facilities. New construction rarely poses a problem, but it can be a challenge to retrofit an existing facility. OSPB exceptions may be granted by the Assistant Secretary for Diplomatic Security. If an exception to an OSPB standard is needed, the requestor must explain the justification for such an exception. All areas that fall short of the required standards must be identified and mitigating measures must be described to explain how the facility will address the shortfall.

There are times when U.S. national interests require our immediate presence. In these circumstances, we must find a suitable facility and enhance security to the maximum extent possible. Time and the limits of construction feasibility circumscribe our ability to retrofit an existing structure to meet our full standards. In the future, secure expedient facilities will likely remain a critical need, and we continue to examine how to best meet this need based on the totality of the operating environment and host country capabilities.

Question. According to testimony from Secretary Clinton before the committee, she and other senior leaders at the Department were never briefed on pleas from Ambassador Stevens for increased security personnel. Specifically, the Secretary, when asked whether she participated in meetings regarding the deteriorating security in Libya, she stated that ". . . with specific security requests, they did not come to me. I had no knowledge of them." The Secretary also testified that "the ARB made very clear that the level of responsibility for the failures that they outlined was set at the Assistant Secretary level and below."

- Under the new procedures the Department put in place after the Benghazi attacks, what are the specific roles and decisionmaking requirements, if any, of each of the top three officials at State (Secretary, Deputy Secretary, and Under Secretary for Management) for addressing security requests and crises at high-risk, high-threat posts, like in Benghazi, and how will that role and involvement in decisionmaking be documented?

Answer. Decisions on security requests from posts are made by consultation within the Department. Working with Regional Security Officers and other officials at posts, Deputy Assistant Secretaries of the Regional Bureaus, their staff, Department leadership, and the Bureau of Diplomatic Security interact daily to ensure that threats and security needs not only at the high-threat, high-risk posts, but worldwide, receive the appropriate scrutiny and response. Secretary Kerry has noted that we can never provide a 100-percent risk-free operating environment. Nevertheless, the Department is determined to take measures to mitigate risks whenever and wherever possible. The Department works every day to balance security with the ability of our diplomats to get out and do their jobs.

We are working to ensure that our risk-management process for high-threat locations is institutionalized, repeatable, and transparent. Reviews of the U.S. Government presence and mission, and our security posture, will take place at least annually following the update of the high-threat, high-risk posts list. This process will also provide for such reviews on an ad hoc basis in the event the security situation in a location deteriorates.

This review for each location determined to be a high-threat, high-risk post will be documented via a memorandum approved by the highest levels of the Department.

Question. Based on briefings and information provided by the State Department, we understand that OMB rejected the Department's $950 million proposal for a consolidated facility and directed the Department to undertake a review of existing training capabilities associated costs.

• Is that process completed, and if so, and what has been determined?

Answer. Because of the ongoing, serious fiscal challenges facing the U.S. Government, including the order of sequestration, which went into effect on March 1, the administration asked the General Services Administration (GSA) and the Department of State (DOS) to perform additional due diligence to determine the best use of taxpayer funds. As a result, the Department is conducting additional cost studies for the Foreign Affairs Security Training Center (FASTC) project. The Department has also been asked to work with the Department of Homeland Security (DHS) to evaluate whether any training capacity for DOS personnel is available at the Federal Law Enforcement Training Center (FLETC) in Glynco, GA. Further work on the FASTC project at Fort Pickett has been put on hold, pending the results of the additional due diligence effort with FLETC.

Based on information FLETC has provided to date, the Department does not believe FLETC has excess training capacity available to provide the necessary and timely platform for a dedicated DOS training facility. DOS continues to support Fort Pickett as the best location to build FASTC. The Department is committed to an open and transparent process and will provide more information to the committee as it becomes available and decisions are made regarding the future of FASTC.

Question. Is there no combination of existing government or private sector training facilities (including but not limited to federal law enforcement training centers and DOD facilities like the Naval Support Activity Charleston) that could be combined to provide the same training that a brand-new FASTC facility would provide?

Answer. Since 2009, the Department of State and the General Services Administration (GSA) have invested considerable time and effort in reviewing over 70 properties, including the Department of Defense (DOD) facilities and law enforcement facilities before identifying 1,500 acres of land on and near Fort Pickett, an under-utilized military base located in Blackstone, VA, that meet our specific requirements for a hard-skills training facility.

Over the last 2 years, the Department of State and GSA have worked extensively to conduct environmental studies, start negotiations for land use agreements, secure community support at Fort Pickett, and ultimately reassess the scope of the FASTC project at Fort Pickett. Through these efforts, it was determined that a smaller platform at Fort Pickett was more fiscally prudent.

The proximity of Fort Pickett, which allows the Department to maintain and strengthen synergies due to its proximity to Department Headquarters, the National Foreign Affairs Training Center (also known as the Foreign Service Institute), DOD, and the Intelligence Community (IC), cannot be overstated. The evolving overseas mission and continually changing worldwide security environment requires greater coordination with our partners, particularly DOD on the ''new normal,'' and positioning FASTC at Fort Pickett will allow the Department to meet this need well into the future.

Question. Has the State Department requested, initiated, or completed any internal or external cost analyses of its different options for future training of diplomatic personnel, including an analysis of alternatives like using existing government or private sector facilities? If the answer is yes, please provide any and all materials indicating or discussing these cost analyses, including any internal correspondence discussing cost analyses, whether or not such analyses were ever completed.

Answer. Since 2009, the General Services Administration (GSA) and the Department of State (DOS) have undertaken an extensive process in the search for a possible site for the proposed Foreign Affairs Security Training Center (FASTC). Over 70 sites have been evaluated for their potential to meet the needs of the security and law enforcement training for the State Department. Project costs, as well as socioeconomic and environmental impacts are just a few of the many variables evaluated as part of the site selection process.

Currently, security and law enforcement training functions for the State Department are conducted in approximately 19 separate leased and contracted training facilities dispersed around the country. The fact that the existing training facilities are widely geographically separated creates difficulties in managing and coordinating activities. Additionally, because the existing training facilities are located in leased space or contracted facilities, the Bureau of Diplomatic Security (DS) must modify or adjust training to fit within the limitations of the facility. The lack of a dedicated training facility also results in scheduling inefficiencies, increased costs, and decreased productivity. DS security and law enforcement training courses often need to be postponed or canceled at the existing training facilities as they must compete for time and space with other Federal agencies' activities, including training requirements of the military. In addition, there are very few commercially available training centers to accommodate the specialized training needs of DS. The development of the FASTC would establish a consolidated hard-skills training center from which DS could efficiently conduct training for a wide array of participants, including the foreign affairs community and DS personnel to meet increased demand for well-trained personnel. Consolidation would also meet the directives of a June 2010 Presidential Memorandum, "Disposing of Unneeded Federal Real Estate," which directs U.S. Government agencies to eliminate lease arrangements that are not cost effective and to pursue consolidation of operations.

As part of the Master Planning process, the Department of State and GSA developed a detailed cost estimate to construct FASTC at Fort Pickett. Additionally, a socioeconomic impact analysis was completed as part of the Draft Environmental Impact Statement. This analysis indicated a substantial economic benefit would be realized by Ft. Pickett/Nottoway County, and the surrounding area.

Because of the ongoing, serious fiscal challenges facing the U.S. Government, including the order of sequestration, which went into effect on March 1, the administration asked GSA and the Department to perform additional due diligence to determine the best use of taxpayer funds. Accordingly, the Department reassessed the scope of the FASTC project; determining a smaller, hard-skills-only training platform at Fort Pickett was more fiscally prudent. Preliminary estimates indicate that project construction costs could be reduced by approximately $375 million to $461 million. Additionally, the annual per-student cost could be reduced by over 50 percent compared to the cost of current hard-skills training methodologies.

The Department is happy to provide a briefing on the FASTC Project, including cost estimates and cost benefit analysis.

Question. What contingency plans were in place for Benghazi?

Answer. As the independent Accountability Review Board on Benghazi noted in their report, following the initiation of the attack on the Special Mission Complex (SMC), the Diplomatic Security Agents immediately reacted according to their emergency plan. " Following the SMC's emergency plan, Assistant Regional Security Officer (ARSO) 1 entered Villa C to secure the Ambassador and the Information Management Officer (IMO) in the safe area and to retrieve his kit; ARSOs 2, 3, and 4 moved to retrieve their kits, which were located in Villa B and the Tactical Operations Comman (TOC) . . . From Villa C, ARSO 4 ran to his sleeping quarters in Villa B to retrieve his kit, while ARSOs 2 and 3 ran to the TOC, where ARSO 3 had last seen the Ambassador, and where ARSO 2's kit was located." (ARSO 2's sleeping quarters were in the TOC, making him the designated "TOC Officer" in their emergency react plan.) Additionally, the Regional Security Office was responsible for planning and conducting evacuation operations of Chief of Mission personnel in the event of a significant attack or substantial deterioration of local security. As such, the office had developed a written evacuation plan which depending on security conditions and specific threat information may have meant the evacuation of personnel from the compound to the Annex, to the east toward Tobruk or from the country entirely.

Because of the tumultuous conditions and natural disasters faced periodically around the world, the Department has robust contingency planning at all posts; this planning involves the interagency, including the Department of Defense. Generally, when the Department is faced with evacuating post personnel, we seek to inform private U.S. citizens in that country, under a "no double standard" policy, and may urge our citizens to leave the country. Typically, U.S. Government employees and citizens will leave via commercial aircraft; on occasion we have asked airlines to add flights to their schedules. If commercial aircraft are not available or lack capacity, we have a process in place to charter aircraft. Our third option is military aircraft; DOD is always receptive to any Department requests.

U.S. diplomatic missions maintain an Emergency Action Committee (EAC), which is comprised of members of the country team, including DOD elements present at post. The EAC is chaired by the Deputy Chief of Mission and validated by the Chief of Mission. The EAC also reviews security policies, such as post's travel policy, which may recommend particular modes of transport and prohibited times and/or locations of travel, and develops post's Emergency Action Plan (EAP). The EAC must review the capabilities and limitations that may impact post's ability to operate, to communicate with the private U.S. citizen community, and to carry out post plans in response to a crisis.

In addition, the Crisis Management Training (CMT) division of State's Foreign Service Institute provides training in crisis management and emergency preparedness for over 100 overseas posts each year. The CMT division's mission is to help prepare U.S. Government employees and teams operating within the foreign affairs community to effectively respond before, during, and in the aftermath of all crises. The CMT division distributes guidance on lessons learned and best practices developed from past crises; provides example EAPs; and has developed distance learning courses for Crisis Management.

Question. Were these contingency plans implemented when the Benghazi compound was attacked, and if so, what went wrong?

Answer. Emergency react plans were implemented as the Accountability Review Board on Benghazi noted in their report: "Following the SMC's emergency plan, Assistant Regional Security Officer (ARSO) 1 entered Villa C to secure the Ambassador and the Information Management Officer (IMO) in the safe area and to retrieve his kit; ARSOs 2, 3, and 4 moved to retrieve their kits, which were located in Villa B and the Tactical Operations Command (TOC) . . . From Villa C, ARSO 4 ran to his sleeping quarters in Villa B to retrieve his kit, while ARSOs 2 and 3 ran to the TOC, where ARSO 3 had last seen the Ambassador, and where ARSO 2's kit was located." (ARSO 2's sleeping quarters were in the TOC, making him the designated "TOC Officer" in their emergency react plan.) The report further states, "Around the same time, the temporary duty (TDY) Regional Security Officer (RSO) working in the TOC heard shots and an explosion. He then saw via security camera dozens of individuals, many armed, begin to enter the compound through the main entrance at the C1 gate. He hit the duck-and-cover alarm and yelled a warning over the radio, and recalled no such warning from the February 17 or Blue Mountain Libya (BML) guards, who had already begun to flee to points south and east in the compound, toward the Villa B area. ARSOs 1 and 2 heard an attack warning from the BML guards passed on over the radio. The TDY RSO also alerted the Annex and Embassy Tripoli by cell phone."

The Regional Security Office in Benghazi was responsible for planning and conducting evacuation operations of Chief of Mission personnel in the event of a significant attack or substantial deterioration of local security. As such, the office had developed a written evacuation plan which depending on security conditions and specific threat information may have meant the evacuation of personnel from the Benghazi compound to the Annex, to the east toward Tobruk, Libya or from the country entirely. Additionally, if it was determined an attack warranted the full evacuation of the compound, RSO staff "will contact the Annex and notify them of the intention to relocate."

With respect to coordination with the Annex, the ARB weighed in by noting that "just prior to receiving the TDY RSO's distress call shortly after 21:42 local time, the head of Annex security heard multiple explosions coming from the north in the direction of the SMC. The Annex security head immediately began to organize his team's departure and notified his superiors, who began to contact local security elements to request support. The Annex response team departed its compound in two vehicles at approximately 22:05 local time. The departure of the Annex team was not delayed by orders from superiors; the team leader decided on his own to depart the Annex compound once it was apparent, despite a brief delay to permit their continuing efforts, that rapid support from local security elements was not forthcoming."

The interagency also worked quickly and collaboratively to respond to the attack in Benghazi on September 11, and the ARB stated that "Washington-Tripoli-

Benghazi communication, cooperation, and coordination on the night of the attacks were effective. . . ."

The ARB further went on to state "The interagency response was timely and appropriate, but there simply was not enough time given the speed of the attacks for armed U.S. military assets to have made a difference. Senior-level interagency discussions were underway soon after Washington received initial word of the attacks and continued through the night. The Board found no evidence of any undue delays in decisionmaking or denial of support from Washington or from the military combatant commanders. Quite the contrary: the safe evacuation of all U.S. Government personnel from Benghazi 12 hours after the initial attack and subsequently to Ramstein Air Force Base was the result of exceptional U.S. Government coordination and military response and helped save the lives of two severely wounded Americans."

The Department is working more closely to coordinate with the Department of Defense and other interagency colleagues as we adjust our posture in light of the new landscape we face today around the world. However, operating overseas presents unique challenges, and there is never a complete guarantee of safety—but in the face of ever-evolving threats, the Department strives to provide the most secure environment possible for the conduct of America's foreign policy.

Question. Why would an independent review by the inspector general regarding the Department's contingency planning be of concern to the Department?

Answer. The Department has no concerns with independent review by the inspector general of any of the Departments operations. The Department appreciates the recommendations of the Office of the Inspector General (OIG) in their audits and inspections of our various bureaus, offices, and programs. We take all reports and recommendations seriously, prioritize the OIG findings and address the corresponding recommendations accordingly.

Question. Please explain the coordination between the State Department and Department of Defense in coordinating drills at U.S. overseas posts as it pertains to Fleet Antiterrorism Security Teams also known as FAST. How often are these drills conducted?

Answer. A robust training program is essential for emergency preparedness. Providing post personnel with skill sets and essential information for emergency situations leads to an efficient and cohesive response to emergencies. The post's Emergency Action Committee is responsible for conducting drills, including their preparation, execution, and evaluation. Drills provide an opportunity to practice and evaluate the responses to emergencies. Emergency Action Committees are compromised of representatives of all U.S. Government agencies at post, including when applicable, Department of Defense representation.

The Marine Security Guard (MSG) Detachment, led by the Regional Security Officer (RSO), is trained to respond to an array of contingencies and many of these are practiced in set drills. These drills include: internal defense, fire, bomb, mass casuality, emergency destruction, and intruder. Drills are conducted on an established schedule and must be reported to the Department per established policy.

Coordination of training with other United States Marine Corps (USMC) elements such as USMC Fleet Antiterrorism Security Team (FAST) or USMC Marine Expeditionary Unit (MEU) are facilitated by the Bureau of Diplomatic Security (DS) routinely in training scenarios in the continental United States (CONUS) and occasionally in theater. In CONUS, DS Special Agents with overseas experience are called upon to brief MEU personnel prior to deployment. DS Special Agents are involved in a yearly contingency exercise with the Quantico-based USMC Expeditionary Warfare School and DS Special Agents engage with the MEUs as role players in table top exercises. Forward deployed USMC elements are also provided exposure to DS and embassy security contingency planning through geographic command theater exercises. A DS Special Agent (LNO) is assigned to each geographic command and is involved in joint-planning and exercise of contingency plans. Most frequently, DS LNOs are involved in rehearsal of concept and broader theater exercises that target the prospect of noncombatant evacuation planning.

When FAST has been deployed to U.S. diplomatic facilities, it falls under the operational control of the Chief of Mission through the RSO. When the RSO conducts drills with the MSG Detachment and with mission staff, the RSO familiarizes the FAST with the drill scenarios and enlists the FAST participation in some level or aspect of the mission drill.

Question. What is the step-by-step process by which FAST assistance is requested, approved, deployed?

Answer. The Department of State requests military assistance through official correspondence between the Executive Secretaries of the Department of State and Department of Defense. When requesting such assistance, the Department of State defers to the Department of Defense to determine the appropriate type and level of assistance necessary. The Department of State refers the Senator to the Department of Defense for information in the decisionmaking process to approve or deploy FASTs.

Question. How many current Bureau of Diplomatic Security (DS) personnel have criminal records?

Answer. DS agents undergo a background investigation and have been determined suitable for the position and issued a security clearance prior to employment. In addition, they go through clearance reinvestigations every 5 years. Federal security clearances are governed by Executive Order 12968, and adjudicated under the ''Government-wide Adjudicative Guidelines for Determining Eligibility for Access to Classified Information.'' Adjudicative Guideline J-Criminal Conduct is one of the 13 guidelines used in making an access determination. That guideline provides that security concerns may be raised, and a person may be disqualified from holding a security clearance, for a single serious crime or multiple lesser offenses. The guideline also lists conditions that could mitigate security concerns:

(a) So much time has elapsed since the criminal behavior occurred, or it occurred under such unusual circumstances that it is unlikely to recur or does not cast doubt on the individual's reliability, trustworthiness, or good judgment;

(b) The person was pressured or coerced into committing the act and those pressures are no longer present in the person's life;

(c) Evidence that the person did not commit the offense; and

(d) There is evidence of successful rehabilitation; including but not limited to the passage of time without recurrence of criminal activity, remorse or restitution, job training or higher education, good employment record, or constructive community involvement.

These considerations, and others, are taken into account when determining whether a prospective DS agent with a criminal record should receive a clearance, and whether a current agent should maintain their clearance if an offense is committed. Each case is judged on its own merits. It is important to note that an offense that might result in a criminal record could include, but is not limited to, jaywalking, public intoxication, shop lifting, and driving under the influence.

We can determine that since entering the Department, 46 of the 1,930 DS agents (less than 2 percent of agents) have been arrested at some point over the course of their career. The criminal records for these individuals are mostly alcohol or domestic incident related. If a DS agent commits a misdemeanor offense, the Department determines the nature of the security concern and whether it can be mitigated. An agent who is convicted of a felony will lose their security clearance, and disciplinary action will be taken to remove them from their position. Furthermore, all Department employees, including those in DS, must immediately report information of a potentially derogatory nature, including adverse involvement with law enforcement agencies, to the Director, Office of Personnel Security and Suitability. Depending on the nature of that involvement, it could lead to the suspension and revocation of the employee's security clearance.

Question. How many current DS personnel are not permitted to engage in sensitive assignments because of their prior criminal records or involvement?

Answer. Currently, 3 of the 1,930 Bureau of Diplomatic Security (DS) Special Agents have been removed from law enforcement duties due to criminal charges or pending charges, or nonfelony convictions during their employment with DS.

Question. How many current DS personnel have been removed from sensitive assignments or other duties because of misconduct or other inappropriate workplace behaviors?

Answer. Currently, 19 of the 1,930 Bureau of Diplomatic Security (DS) Special Agents have been removed from sensitive assignments or other duties because of misconduct or other inappropriate workplace behaviors.

Question. How many DS personnel have been terminated or relieved of duties because of post-hire revelations of prior criminal records or involvement?

Answer. We have reviewed records for the last 5 years and find that no DS personnel have been terminated or relieved of duties based on prior criminal records or involvement.

Question. Are individuals with criminal records legally eligible to work for DS?

Answer. In most circumstances, individuals with criminal records are not automatically barred from working for the Bureau of Diplomatic Security. There are a number of ways, however, in which a criminal record may render an individual ineligible to serve as a Diplomatic Security Special Agent.

The existence of a criminal record may result in the denial of a federal security clearance, which is a prerequisite for a variety of positions with the Federal Government, including DS Special Agents, who are required at hiring to be eligible to be granted access to Top Secret/Sensitive Compartmented information (TS/SCI). DS Special Agents also are sworn Federal Law enforcement officers and must be eligible to possess a firearm. The Lautenberg amendment to the Gun Control Act, 18 U.S.C. § 922, states a person convicted of a felony or misdemeanor crime of domestic violence may not possess a firearm, which would also bar employment as a Diplomatic Security Special Agent.

In addition, candidates for DS Special Agent positions must pass a suitability review. DS works under the direction of the Bureau of Human Resources Office of Recruitment, Examinations, and Employment (HR/REE) in the recruitment and assessment of DS Special Agents.

If agent candidates pass all phases of pre-employment screening/testing (application prescreening, written and oral assessments), they are given a conditional offer of employment and provided with the security and medical clearance paperwork. Once clearances are obtained, candidates will undergo the final suitability review process. Candidates must pass the final suitability review before being placed on the hiring register and assigned an entrance on duty date.

The final suitability panel consists of two members—an examiner from HR/REE and a former Special Agent subject-matter-expert from DS. Both panel members review the reports of investigation prepared by the Office of Personnel Security and Suitability (DS/SI/PSS) and make a suitability determination, based on the Final Review Panel (FRP) criteria. If the panel members are not in agreement, the HR/REE Director assigns a third individual to serve as the tie breaker. If the candidate fails the final suitability review, their candidacy is terminated.

Terminated candidates may appeal a finding of unsuitability. Appeals must be submitted in writing within 60 days of receiving a denial letter, or the candidate must request an extension in writing from the HR/REE Director. As outlined in the FRP denial letter, an appeal must provide new or additional information that specifically addresses the grounds for denial as laid out in the letter, which clearly indicates that the panel's decision was based on inaccurate information, and thus was in error. An appeals panel consisting of two assessors with no previous contact with the case will adjudicate appeals.

In adjudicating the case, the panel is limited in its review to the reasons for the initial denial of suitability cited in the letter to the candidate and must base its decision only on the new information provided by the candidate in the appeal. The chair of the panel will draft a report of findings, and the approval or denial letter for the HR/REE Director's signature. If the panel fails to reach consensus, the HR/REE Director will make the final determination.

In assessing candidates' suitability, the panel applies the Department's Standards for Appointment and Continued Suitability, which are set out in the Foreign Affairs Manual (FAM). The FAM 4130 states that "criminal, dishonest, or disgraceful conduct" may constitute grounds for disqualifying an applicant based on suitability. During the suitability review, the panel considers such factors as criminal history, past drug or alcohol abuse, and misconduct in prior employment. Although a past criminal violation does not automatically disqualify a person for service, it would be a strong indicator against employment and would be scrutinized intently, considering the nature of the offense, the age when it occurred, and any extenuating circumstances. Because DS Special Agents serve as law enforcement officers, they are held to a higher standard than other applicants and their suitability review is more stringent.

Question. Is DS functionally a federal law enforcement agency?

Answer. Yes. To counter global threats, the Office of the Chief Special Agent, the forerunner of diplomatic security, was formed in 1916. It was not until 1985, in the aftermath of the Beirut bombings, that DS became a Bureau within the State Department. Diplomatic Security (DS) Special Agents are sworn federal law enforcement officers who are responsible for the security of U.S. Government personnel, property, and sensitive information throughout the world. DS Special Agents are also responsible for the protection of the Secretary of State, certain foreign dignitaries visiting the United States, and others as designated by the Secretary of State. Major activities include protective services, management of security programs for Foreign Service posts, criminal investigations, and background investigations.

The Diplomatic Security Service operates under several statutory authorities, including: The Omnibus Diplomatic Security Act, signed in 1986, which is the basic authorizing legislation. Under this act, the Secretary of State has responsibility to develop policies and programs for the protection of all U.S. Government personnel, including military personnel who fall under Chief of Mission authority, on official duty abroad; security at U.S. diplomatic missions abroad; and security at State Department facilities in the United States.

In addition, 22 U.S.C. § 2709 provides Special Agents of the Diplomatic Security Service with the authority to conduct criminal investigations concerning passport or visa fraud. DS agents have the statutory authority to protect visiting foreign dignitaries, the Secretary of State, and other official representatives of the U.S. Government as directed. The statute also gives DS agents the authority to carry firearms and to obtain and execute federal search and arrest warrants.

The National Intelligence Reform Act gives DS the lead authority in the United States for developing a plan to stop U.S. visa and passport fraud worldwide. In April 2005, a new law was signed by President George W. Bush, which expanded legal authorities for DS agents. DS Agents are also authorized to make arrests without a warrant for any federal offense committed in their presence or for probable cause. These expanded authorities are a tremendous benefit to DS agents in that they immediately enhance DS's effectiveness in fulfilling its critical law enforcement role.

Question. Have any State Department personnel ever instructed any DS personnel or other State Department personnel to make exceptions to otherwise applicable hiring rules and regulations, or otherwise take any actions outside the normal course of their duties, with respect to the hiring of an individual with a criminal record to work in DS? If the answer is yes, please provide their names and all correspondence and documents related to such requests.

Answer. No; there is no record that any State Department personnel have ever instructed any DS personnel or other State Department personnel to make exceptions to otherwise applicable hiring rules and regulations, or otherwise take any actions outside the normal course of their duties, with respect to hiring an individual with a criminal record to work in DS.

Question. Please provide a detailed analysis comparing the benefits State Department personnel would receive under S. 980, as introduced (e.g., death gratuity, supplemental life insurance, survivors education, intern gratuities, and retroactive payments) to comparable benefits for:
    (a) Current FSO benefits;
    (b) Benefits for DOD service members;
    (c) Benefits for federal employees in the intelligence community serving overseas; and
    (d) Benefits for other non-FSO federal civilian employees.
Please include in this analysis the amounts paid into any such benefit programs by each category of beneficiaries.

Answer (a). The death gratuity and associated benefits that are payable to the designated beneficiaries of a Department of State employee who is killed in the line of duty are highly variable, and depend largely on such factors as the employee's current salary, total years of creditable service, the total life insurance coverage selected, the number of surviving dependents, and how long the survivors live to collect benefits. The various benefits and options available can be found in the attached tab regarding compensation available to families of Foreign Service and Civil Service Employees.

Answer (b). As of July 2012, our understanding of the broad outlines of certain relevant Department of Defense benefits to service members is as follows:

Death Gratuity: $100,000 or one year's salary, whichever is greater
Burial Costs: up to $8,800
Insurance: $400,000
Educational Benefit: $936 per month for full-time attendance (per spouse/child) [up to 45 months]
Children (per child): $486 per month (up to age 22 if still in school)
Social Security Benefits: [per SSA entitlement]
Pension: average of 3 high salary x 75% x 55%

We refer you to the Department of Defense for more detailed information.

Answer (c). The Department of State does not possess this information. We refer you to the individual agencies, which would be better positioned to provide the information.

Answer (d). The chart provided in the attached tab also discusses the benefits available to Civil Service employees, regardless of agency (only Title 22 authorizations are limited to the Foreign Service). We refer you to individual agencies for additional information.

ATTACHMENT:

COMPENSATION THAT MAY BE PROVIDED TO ELIGIBLE FAMILIES OF DECEASED U.S. PERSONNEL: U.S. FOREIGN SERVICE (FS) EMPLOYEES, CIVIL SERVICE (CS) EMPLOYEES, AND FOR THOSE EMPLOYEES KILLED IN THE LINEOF DUTY AND/OR A TERRORIST INCIDENT

FECA5 U.S.C 8133–8137.	Central benefit: Surviving spouse receives monthly— 50% of employee's salary; if dependent children, 45% of salary plus additional 15% for each child up to a total of 75% of salary.	Reductions: Monthly survivor benefits are reduced if: employee was covered under FERS or FSPS and survivors receive SS benefits based on deceased's Federal employment.	Length of survivor benefits: Tax-free spousal monthly benefit is paid for life or until remarriage if before age 55.	Funeral or burial expenses: Contingent upon written approval by DOL. Usually, several months are required for processing. DOL pays up to $800 to personal representative. DOL pays up to $200 to personal representative.
Retirement benefits.	Survivor annuity: Paid based on applicable retirement system: FERS, CSRS, FSRDS, FSPS. Not payable if FECA payments are made.	Election choice: If FECA benefit is chosen over retirement annuity, survivors may receive a lump sum payment of the deceased's contributions to relevant retirement fund.	FECA benefit: Most survivors choose FECA benefits because FECA pays a higher amount and are tax exempt.	
Social Security.	Survivor benefits: Payable to qualifying surviving spouses and dependent children. Dependent parents and former spouses may qualify.	Benefit Amount: Lump sum of $255 is payable to qualifying surviving spouse. If no qualifying spouse, lump sum is paid to children eligible for benefits. Otherwise no lump sum is payable.	Benefit condition: Amount depends on SS earnings and number of survivors eligible for benefits.	
Title VI, Section 651 of Public Law 104–208 (The Omnibus Consolidated Appropriations Act of 1996).	Death Gratuity (for funeral and burial expenses): Up to $10,000 payable to personal representative of deceased employee.	Reduction: Payment must be reduced by amount of DOL payment toward funeral and administrative expenses (up to $1,000).	Benefit reality: Since FECA typically pays out $1,000 for funeral and administrative expenses, State's death gratuity payment is usually $9,000 and is taxable. FECA provision (*8102a) cited below effective 1/2008 increased the death gratuity payment up to a maximum of $100,000 offset by other death gratuities paid out.	

COMPENSATION THAT MAY BE PROVIDED TO ELIGIBLE FAMILIES OF DECEASED U.S. PERSONNEL: U.S. FOREIGN SERVICE (FS) EMPLOYEES, CIVIL SERVICE (CS) EMPLOYEES, AND FOR THOSE EMPLOYEES KILLED IN THE LINEOF DUTY AND/OR A TERRORIST INCIDENT—Continued

*FECA 8102a (Section 1105 of Public Law 110–181) January 2009.	Death gratuity: The USG pays a death gratuity of up to $100,000 to or for the survivor prescribed by subsection (d) immediately upon receiving official notification of the death of an employee who dies of injuries incurred in connection with the employee's service with an Armed Force in a contingency operation.	Benefit Amount: The death gratuity payable under this section shall be reduced by the amount of any death gratuity provided under section 413 of the Foreign Service Act of 1980, section 1603 of the Emergency Supplemental Appropriations Act for Defense, the Global War on Terror, and Hurricane Recovery, 2006 [unclassified], or any other law of the United States based on the same death.	Beneficiary Reality and Form: For an employee who has no surviving spouse or child and is eligible to receive the death gratuity, the employee may designate any one or more of his/her parents or brothers or sisters to receive specific shares of the gratuity.	
Section 413 of Foreign Service Act, 22 U.S.C. 3973.	Death gratuity: Payment equal to one year's salary of the employee at the time of death. Surviving dependents of Federal employee who dies as a result of injuries sustained in the performance of duty abroad.	Recipient: Surviving dependents of Federal employee who die as a result of injuries sustained in the performance of duty abroad.	Condition: Death must be first accepted by DOL, in writing, with qualifying FECA provision noted, before State can authorize payment.	Complications: Processing by DOL may take several months. Complications should be expected if terrorism or foul play is involved. Nexus between death and employment must be established.
Victims of Terrorism Compensation Act, 5 U.S.C 5570 and 22 CFR 192.	Benefit: Payment provided if President (through DOJ–FBI) determines that death was caused by hostile action and resulted from individual's relationship with the Government.	Reduction: Payment must be reduced by any other amount payable by USG in connection with death or disability.	Benefit Reality: Because of other payment authorized above, including FECA and Section 413 of FS Act authorizing 1-year salary, this benefit is rarely paid because of the offset provision of the law.	Delegated Authority: Secretary of State, in consultation with the Secretary of Labor. Department regulation provides death benefit payment for either an employee or a family member of an employee is equal to 1 year's salary of the principal at the time of death.

COMPENSATION THAT MAY BE PROVIDED TO ELIGIBLE FAMILIES OF DECEASED U.S. PERSONNEL: U.S. FOREIGN SERVICE (FS) EMPLOYEES, CIVIL SERVICE (CS) EMPLOYEES, AND FOR THOSE EMPLOYEES KILLED IN THE LINEOF DUTY AND/OR A TERRORIST INCIDENT—Continued

Income Tax Relief 26 U.S.C. 692.	Federal Income Tax: Not applicable, if death resulted from injury incurred outside the U.S. in a terrorist or military action for the tax year of the death and any prior taxable year in the period beginning with the last taxable year ending before the year in which the injury was incurred.			
Life Insurance: Federal Employees Group Life Insurance (FEGLI).	Payment: Basic Life Insurance equal to an employee's rate of annual basic pay (rounded to the next $1,000) plus $2,000, or $10,000, whichever is greater. USG Payment: ⅓ of the cost of Basic Insurance.	Optional Insurance benefits: Employees may also be entitled to additional optional coverage payment, if employee elected it before death and paid the full cost of Optional Insurance.	Accidental Death: Pays additional benefits for those who elected Basic Life Insurance and Option A.	Beneficiary: Unless employee designates a specific beneficiary, the benefit is paid according to the order of precedence mandated by law. Proceeds of FEGLI policies paid to designated beneficiaries are not taxable as income to the beneficiary.
Federal Employees Health Benefits Program (FEHBP).	Eligibility: Eligible survivors may continue enrollment if deceased employee was enrolled for self and family at the time of death.	Condition: At least one family member is entitled to a monthly annuity as the survivor of the deceased employee.		
Thrift Savings Plan (TSP).	Payment: Employee's TSP accounts are distributed according to the employee's Designation of Beneficiary form.	Federal Tax: To postpone paying federal tax, all or any part of the payment may be made to an IRA.		
Unpaid Compensation (Final pay and unused Annual Leave).	Payment: Designated survivor(s) of USG employee who are killed may receive lump sum-payment covering final pay and unused annual leave from the employee's agency.			

41

COMPENSATION THAT MAY BE PROVIDED TO ELIGIBLE FAMILIES OF DECEASED U.S. PERSONNEL:
U.S. FOREIGN SERVICE (FS) EMPLOYEES, CIVIL SERVICE (CS) EMPLOYEES, AND FOR THOSE
EMPLOYEES KILLED IN THE LINEOF DUTY AND/OR A TERRORIST INCIDENT—Continued

Emergencies in the Diplomatic and Consular Services Authority.	Payment: Section 4 of the Department of State Basic Authorities Act, 22 U.S.C. 2671, provides that the Secretary is authorized to make expenditures for "unforeseen emergencies arising in the diplomatic and consular service.	Past Practice: DOS used this authority to make expenditures related to the Nairobi bombing.	Collective Expenses: DOS paid for collective expenses on behalf of all American victims (ie., costs of arrival ceremony of surviving family members, meeting for families, and 1-year anniversary commemoration ceremonies).	Payments to families: DOS used this authority for airfare, local transportation, lodging, and other miscellaneous expenses associated with the arrival ceremony, funeral arrangements, and anniversary commemorations.

Revised November 2011

www.ingramcontent.com/pod-product-compliance
Lightning Source LLC
Chambersburg PA
CBHW080627290526
45790CB00007B/2957